THE
PANAMA
CANAL
TRANSFER

THE
PANAMA
CANAL
TRANSFER

CONTROVERSY
AT THE CROSSROADS

SUSAN DUDLEY GOLD

RSVP

RAINTREE
STECK-VAUGHN
PUBLISHERS
A Steck-Vaughn Company

Austin, Texas

www.steck-vaughn.com

Dedication
To my grandfather, Francis Walton, who served in the U.S. Navy in Panama and who died in Central America

Published by Raintree Steck–Vaughn Publishers, an imprint of Steck–Vaughn Company

Acknowledgments
With grateful appreciation and thanks to Barbara and Robert Melville and General Wallace Nutting for sharing so generously their knowledge, time, anecdotes, and photographs. Without their help, this project would have been far less interesting.

Library of Congress Cataloging-in-Publication Data
Gold, Susan Dudley.
The Panama Canal transfer, controversy at the crossroads / Susan Dudley Gold. — 1st ed.
    p.   cm.
Includes bibliographical references and index.
Summary: Examines the history of the Panama Canal, from its conceptual stage through construction up to today, and discusses its controversial political aspects.
ISBN 0-8172-5762-4
1. Panama Canal (Panama)—History—Juvenile literature.
2. Panama—Foreign relations—United States—Juvenile literature.
3. United States—Foreign relations—Panama—Juvenile literature.
[1. Panama Canal (Panama)—History.] I. Title.
F1569.C2G62   1999
972.87'5—dc21   98-47196
                                                            CIP
                                                            AC

Printed in the United States of America
10 9 8 7 6 5 4 3 2 1 LB 02 01 00 99 98

Design, Typography, and Setup
Custom Communications, Saco, ME

Illustration and Photo Credits
Cover, front © W. Wayne Lockwood, M.D./Corbis; *Cover, back (U.S. flag image), p. 3,* © 1995, PhotoDisc, Inc.; *pp. 5, 59, 75, 85, 89, 104, 108, 110,* courtesy Robert Melville; *pp. 7* (recreation of Panama Canal Commission graphic), *8t, 8b, 13, 15t, 15b, 22,* © 1998, Susan Gold; *pp. 21,* Aerospace Audiovisual Service (courtesy Gen. Wallace Nutting); *pp. 24, 51, 53,* courtesy Dudley–Walton family; *pp. 30, 34,* North Wind Picture Archives; *p. 45,* © Corbis–Bettmann; *pp. 65, 68, 94,* © UPI/Corbis–Bettmann; *p. 79, 102,* I.L. Maduro Jr.; *97,* B. Purkis (courtesy Gen. Wallace Nutting); *p. 100,* © Reuters/Corbis–Bettmann

CONTENTS

Introduction
HOME AT LAST   9

Chapter 1
CONTRACT FOR CONTROVERSY   11

Chapter 2
BUILDING A CANAL   23

Chapter 3
AMERICANS TAKE OVER   32

Chapter 4
SIMMERING CONFLICTS   47

Chapter 5
RALLYING AROUND THE FLAG   61

Chapter 6
NEGOTIATING A NEW TREATY   71

Chapter 7
FIGHT FOR RATIFICATION   83

Chapter 8
INVASION   96

Chapter 9
COUNTDOWN TO 1999   106

SOURCE NOTES   112
GLOSSARY   119
FOR FURTHER INFORMATION   122
INDEX   125

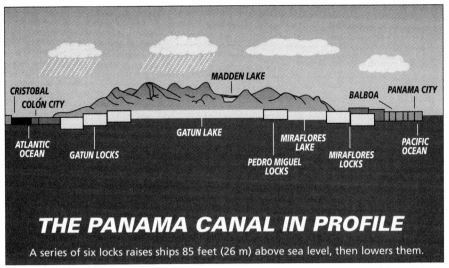

CRISTOBAL
COLÓN CITY
MADDEN LAKE
BALBOA
PANAMA CITY
ATLANTIC
OCEAN
GATUN LOCKS
GATUN LAKE
MIRAFLORES
LAKE
PEDRO MIGUEL
LOCKS
MIRAFLORES
LOCKS
PACIFIC
OCEAN

THE PANAMA CANAL IN PROFILE

A series of six locks raises ships 85 feet (26 m) above sea level, then lowers them.

Source: Panama Canal Commission

Panama Canal Facts

- Most transits in a single day: 65, February 29, 1968.
- Fastest transit: U.S. Navy hydrofoil *Pegasus*, from Miraflores through the Gatun Locks in 2 hours 41 minutes, June 1979.
- Largest user: United States—from October 1994 to September 1995, 90.7 million long tons of cargo originated in the U.S.; 38.1 million tons were destined for the U.S.
- Largest commodity shipped through canal: Grain, at 44.1 million long tons (from October 1994 to September 1995). Petroleum was the second largest and accounted for 14 percent to 17 percent of total canal shipments during fiscal years 1995–1997.
- Number of vessels served: More than 790,000 vessels since 1914.

From the Panama Canal Commission and the U.S. Energy Information Administration

Panama

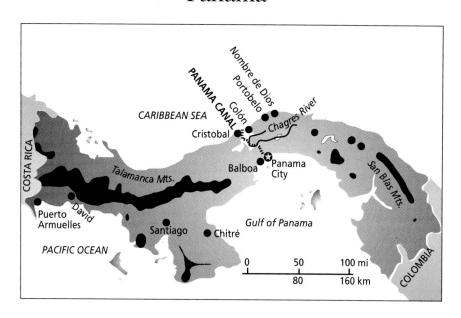

Western Hemisphere

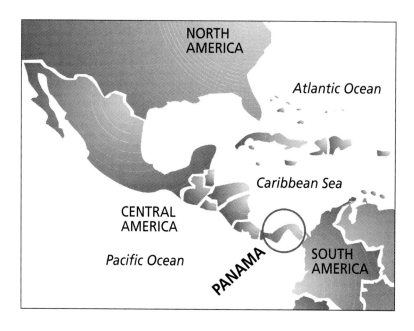

8

Introduction

HOME AT LAST

Ancon Hill, October 1, 1979

Atop the bare crest of 656-foot (200-m) Ancon Hill, delegates from every free-trade nation in the world gather for a momentous ceremony. Far below, the Panama Canal's locks raise and lower massive commercial ships on their way from one ocean to another. Other ships wait to transit the canal in the Bay of Panama, dotted with islands and ringed with lush tropical vegetation. If one looks down the hill's other side, where dense jungle forests hide granite slabs once quarried here for lock construction, Panama City's skyline shows off modern skyscrapers, hotels, and banks that tower over the shanties of the poor. Cars clog the highways; tourists jostle with business people as they pass on city sidewalks.

But this is not a business-as-usual Monday morning. On this day, October 1, 1979, the United States will turn over jurisdiction of the Panama Canal Zone—the 10-mile-wide (16-m)

9

strip of land running 50 miles (80 km) through the center of Panama and surrounding the canal. The 1977 Panama Canal Treaty, ratified by the U.S. Senate by a razor-thin margin in April 1978, becomes effective today. Under the treaty, Panama reclaims its land and embarks on a shared journey with the United States that will end twenty years later when Panama becomes the sole operator/owner of the Panama Canal.

As the world's leaders look on, U.S. Army General Wallace Nutting, commander of the U.S. Southern Command, wearing a bright-white uniform decorated with the ribbons and medals of his rank, signs the documents that officially dissolve the Panama Canal Zone.

Above all, on an aluminum flagpole that pokes its way into the sky, flies an enormous banner the size of three basketball courts. A red and a blue square alternate with two white squares, each with a star at its center—the flag of Panama.

An old Panamanian man looks up at the great flag with pride in his eyes as tears stream down his cheeks. He has never before been allowed to stand on this magnificent promontory, to look down at the vast sweep of land that is his country, Panama. Until this moment, the hill, the flagpole, and the land surrounding the canal have been under the control of the United States. For the first time in seventy-six years, Ancon Hill is under Panama's jurisdiction.[1]

Chapter One

CONTRACT FOR CONTROVERSY

Everyone has been focused on getting the Canal Zone
back from the Americans—as if everything will be
magically fine once that happens. It's not going to be
that easy.[1]

—Stanley Muschett
Panamanian civic leader

Panama's people have waited for almost a century—the country's entire history as an independent nation—to take control of their
homeland. From 1903, when American engineers first
laid out the route the Panama Canal would follow, Panamanians were forced to share their land with a foreign
power. For much of that time, Panamanians couldn't step
foot on soil within the Canal Zone—530 square miles
(1,372 sq km) of land that divided their country in two—
without the permission of the United States.

The passage of the Panama Canal Treaty and the accompanying Neutrality Treaty in 1978 changed all that. At noon, on December 31, 1999, the final vestiges of U.S. control will come to an end. The Panama Canal and the remaining military bases, schools, and administration buildings established by the United States will become the property of the Republic of Panama. An eleven-member board of directors, appointed by the Panamanian president and the legislature, will run the canal.

The Panama Canal Treaty, which sets the terms of the twenty-year canal transfer, will expire on that date. The Neutrality Treaty, guaranteeing that the canal will remain neutral and open to ships of all countries, continues in effect. Under its terms, the United States forever retains the right to defend and protect the canal.

Panama, a small, poor, Central American country about the size of the state of Maine, faces monumental challenges as it assumes control of the canal. Thirteen thousand ships pass through the man-made waterway each year, representing 5 percent of all world trade. Tolls generate $600 million annually. Panama now receives $100 million as its share of the take. Almost all the remaining income is used to maintain and operate the canal. Over the past eighteen years, the canal commission has made little profit despite record-breaking traffic in 1996.[2]

FINANCIAL SHOALS

Panama must negotiate between rocky financial shoals, finding a safe route between expensive repairs and

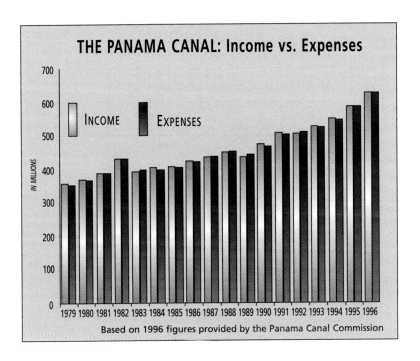

THE PANAMA CANAL: Income vs. Expenses

INCOME EXPENSES

IN MILLIONS

700
600
500
400
300
200
100
0

1979 1980 1981 1982 1983 1984 1985 1986 1987 1988 1989 1990 1991 1992 1993 1994 1995 1996

Based on 1996 figures provided by the Panama Canal Commission

upgrading of the canal on one side and reasonable tolls—used to pay expenses—on the other. Sand and silt must be dredged from the canal to keep it deep enough for the huge vessels that pass through the locks. Equipment, some of it dating back to 1914, must be constantly upgraded and repaired. The Panama Canal Commission, which is in charge of operating the canal until the transfer, has begun widening and deepening the canal, improvements that will cost a total of $1 billion.

If tolls are too high, shippers may find it cheaper to travel the extra 7,872 miles (12,700 km) around Cape Horn rather than using the canal. Even now, some forms of shipping avoid the canal. The largest tankers are too big to fit through the locks and already use alternate routes. Oil is transported via pipeline across Panama. Other shippers deliver their cargoes to U.S. ports, where they are loaded onto trucks and railroad cars and transported across country. Still others make the journey from Atlantic to Pacific by train or truck across Mexico.

An average ship takes about eight to ten hours to pass through the canal. Even with the current improvements, the canal will be able to handle only fifty ships a day. By 2010 or 2015, the canal could have more ships waiting to transit than it can handle. Building a third set of locks to allow larger ships to pass through the canal could cost between $3 billion and $6 billion.

As the countdown nears, observers question whether Panama can operate the canal effectively and efficiently enough to compete. Panama presents a good case for itself. The country's economy has made impressive gains in the last few years. The volume of trade passing through the free-trade zone at Colón, on the Caribbean side of the canal, has reached more than $5 billion annually. Inflation has been held to below 2 percent a year, and bank deposits amounted to more than $4 billion by the early 1990s.[3] Unemployment, still high at 13 percent, has dropped dramatically since the grim days following the U.S. invasion of Panama, when more than a third of Panama's workers couldn't find jobs.

SUEZ SUCCESS

Perhaps Panama's strongest argument lies in the story of another canal a hemisphere away. The Suez Canal in Egypt, built by French engineers and later controlled by the British government, was taken over by Egypt in 1956. The Egyptians have run the canal quite successfully since then except when Egypt's President Gamal Abdel Nasser closed it during the 1967 Arab-Israeli war.

Panama, however, faces several difficulties in taking control of its canal. Only one-fifth of the nation's land is habitable. Jungles and rain forests fill the other four-fifths. Half the country's 2.65 million people live along the canal, concentrated in the capital city, Panama City, and other urban centers on both coasts. More than 40 percent of Panamanian people live in poverty.[4] Slums, barbed wire, and crime are the unfortunate trademarks of the Caribbean city of Colón, Panama's second largest city. More than half of Colón's residents are unemployed.

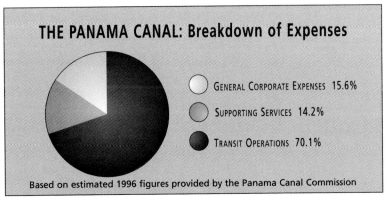

THE PANAMA CANAL: Breakdown of Expenses

General Corporate Expenses 15.6%

Supporting Services 14.2%

Transit Operations 70.1%

Based on estimated 1996 figures provided by the Panama Canal Commission

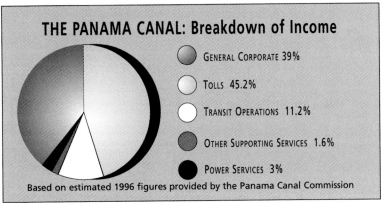

THE PANAMA CANAL: Breakdown of Income

General Corporate 39%

Tolls 45.2%

Transit Operations 11.2%

Other Supporting Services 1.6%

Power Services 3%

Based on estimated 1996 figures provided by the Panama Canal Commission

Panama is a poor credit risk, owing foreign creditors $7.2 billion, more than the country takes in annually (its gross national product).[5]

To help Panama prepare for the task of overseeing the multimillion-dollar enterprise, the transfer of the canal has been a gradual one, stretching over twenty years. When the treaty became effective on October 1, 1979, the Canal Zone and the Panama Canal Company that administered it were dissolved. The Panama Canal Commission, run by a joint board of Americans and Panamanians, now manages the canal and the workers who operate it.

As required by the 1977 treaty, canal administration and operation have gradually shifted from Americans to Panamanians. In 1990, Panamanian Alberto Aleman Zubieta became chair of the Panama Canal Commission, replacing American Joe Reeder in the top post. The Panama Canal Authority, staffed entirely by Panamanians, will replace the commission on December 31, 1999.

More than 90 percent of the canal's 9,400 workers are Panamanians. By 1999, when the canal is turned over to Panama, all employees except a few foreign specialists will be Panamanian citizens. "Nothing will change except the name on the checks to the personnel,"[6] says administrator Zubieta of the upcoming transfer.

Some observers worry that Colombian drug dealers— who have been known to use submarines to transport cocaine through the Caribbean—will try to hold the canal hostage. Just in case, a dam designed to withstand torpedoes, built during World War II to protect the canal, is being revamped at a cost of $12 million. The Neutrality

Treaty gives the United States the right to intervene if necessary to protect the canal from sabotage.

Safety is another concern. Licensing requirements have been reduced for the canal pilots who help guide massive ships—some so large their hulls barely fit in the canal locks—through the waterway. Pilots hired in the days of the U.S.-controlled Panama Canal Company had to hold a master's license and have logged time at sea as ship's captains. Today's pilots are no longer required to have high-seas experience as a captain.[7]

The canal is also threatened by the agricultural practices of Panama's rural farmers. Some cut down forests and burn the land, a method called slash-and-burn agriculture. Such practices lead to erosion and cause water to run off into the sea instead of being absorbed. Both pose problems for the canal. Eroded soil must be constantly dredged out of the waterway. Rain forests catch rain water and store it until it is drained into the canal and used to float ships in the locks. The water supply is crucial because Panama's canal system relies on water to raise and lower ships as they cross from one ocean to the other. Every transit requires more than 50 million gallons (189 million l) of water.

CORRUPTION FEARS

Some observers fear corruption in Panama's government will jeopardize canal operations. Will profits from the canal be used to modernize it, or will they go into the pockets of corrupt government officials and their friends and family? Critics say government-run agencies are inefficient and overburdened with too many workers who hold jobs only because they are relatives or cronies of powerful friends.[8]

Corruption has plagued Panama for decades. Money from drug dealers has lined the pockets of government officials, from deposed dictator Manuel Noriega on down the line. The current president, Ernesto Pérez Balladares, acknowledged in 1997 that drug dealers had given money to his campaign. He said he had not known of the contributions at the time.[9]

Drug lords from Colombia have used Panama banks to "launder" their money—transfer it through the banks so it can't be traced back to illegal drug dealings. In 1990 Panama passed rules to require banks to report large deposits. The laws, based on those in effect in the U.S., are designed to expose drug money, but critics say the illegal money is still flowing through the country.

"Panama's national flag should be a dollar bill with 'Let's make a deal' underneath," says Richard Millet, a history professor and Panama expert. "The deals come in a variety of shapes and sizes, normally crooked."[10]

To guard against unscrupulous politicians, Panamanians added an amendment to their constitution that established a separate, government-owned agency to run the canal. Under the constitution, the Panama Canal Authority—not the president or the legislature—will have direct control over the canal, its employees, tolls collected, and contracts awarded for work to be done at the canal. Each of the eleven members on the board will serve a term of nine years. Their terms will be staggered, so no one group can remain in power. Their activities will be regulated by rules for running the canal passed by the Legislative Assembly (Panama's Congress) in 1997.

Observers greeted the establishment of the separate agency as a good start to ensuring that Panama Canal dealings stay out of the hands of politicians. Their enthusiasm was diluted, however, when President Balladares appointed relatives and political cronies to the board. Balladares' choice for the top position on the board, Jorge Ritter, was Panama's foreign minister under Manuel Noriega, the Panamanian strongman who was deposed from power by U.S. troops in 1989, convicted of drug crimes, and jailed. Balladares and Ritter are both members of the Revolutionary Democratic party (PRD), the political party once led by Noriega.

Balladares also came under fire for his appointment of other board members to the Panama Canal Authority. Among those named to the board are the president's former son-in-law, his cousin, and two of his wife's cousins. He also appointed his campaign-finance chairman and the son of the Minister of Justice. According to Balladares, almost all his appointees already serve on the Panama Canal Commission or have been involved with the canal in other ways.

MAINTENANCE CONCERNS

So far, the transfer has gone smoothly, but observers wonder whether Panama will keep up maintenance on the canal once the Americans are gone. The property Panama took over in 1979 has been neglected for years. Squatters claim the derelict buildings, and once immaculate lawns have become weed-filled vacant lots. The Trans-Isthmus railroad sits unused, its cars and tracks rusted and overgrown.[11]

Carl Posey, who lived in the Canal Zone and returned to the area in 1990, encountered a changed place. Buildings once owned by the U.S. Army and now in the hands of the Panamanian government have crumbled; the once-elegant golf course has become a "shabby" park. Roads are pockmarked with potholes; schools and warehouses abandoned. "Everywhere one looks," Posey writes, "the place is deeply, eternally, in decay, as it has been for decades."[12]

For the first time, Posey saw mosquitoes in the former Zone, a potent reminder of the disease-ridden jungle that existed here before American insect spray and screens took on the deadly carriers of yellow fever and malaria. "The jungle moves in," Posey says, "wherever it can."[13]

"Panama is not known for good maintenance," says Robert Melville, who spent three years in Panama as a member of the Episcopal Church's Volunteers for a Mission program. "The canal's got to be kept in good repair or it won't work."[14]

General Wallace Nutting, the former commander of the U.S. Southern Command in Panama, now retired, has seen similar scenes of dilapidated buildings and encroaching jungle on his return trips to Panama. "It's a worry,"[15] he acknowledges. But he notes that the canal continues to be well-maintained. Rundown buildings and property in the former Canal Zone may look bad, but keeping the canal in good shape is the most important goal.

U.S. General Nutting on field patrol in 1981

Some Panamanians, still resentful over past U.S. intervention, wonder whether Americans are raising doubts about Panama's ability to oversee the canal as a way of reasserting control. The United States does have a keen interest in the continued success of the canal. Fourteen percent of U.S. trade passes through the canal each year. But the waterway and the former Canal Zone are no longer vital to U.S. military interests. The Southern Command, which once directed U.S. military activities in Latin America from headquarters in the Canal Zone, moved to Miami in April 1997. The U.S. Navy, once dependent on the canal to patrol both coasts, now has an Atlantic and a Pacific fleet. Many Navy ships are now too large to fit through the canal's locks.

Panamanians themselves seem unsure about total American withdrawal. A recent poll shows three-fourths of Panama's people want some U.S. troops to remain on the isthmus. Their attitude comes not from nostalgia for the old way of life, but from attachment to the

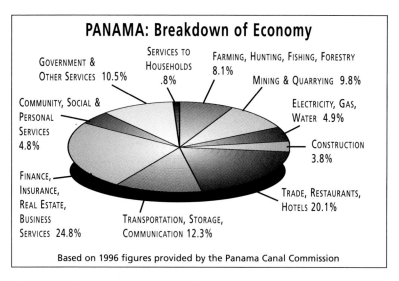

PANAMA: Breakdown of Economy

GOVERNMENT & OTHER SERVICES 10.5%

SERVICES TO HOUSEHOLDS .8%

FARMING, HUNTING, FISHING, FORESTRY 8.1%

MINING & QUARRYING 9.8%

COMMUNITY, SOCIAL & PERSONAL SERVICES 4.8%

ELECTRICITY, GAS, WATER 4.9%

CONSTRUCTION 3.8%

FINANCE, INSURANCE, REAL ESTATE, BUSINESS SERVICES 24.8%

TRANSPORTATION, STORAGE, COMMUNICATION 12.3%

TRADE, RESTAURANTS, HOTELS 20.1%

Based on 1996 figures provided by the Panama Canal Commission

Panama Canal operations and money spent by its employees and their families account for 20 percent of Panama's economy. The revenue is divided among a number of different categories, including trade, finance, and other services.

money spent by U.S. citizens. Americans—civilian canal workers and U.S. soldiers—spend an estimated $370 million in Panama each year.[16]

Panama's president told a reporter for *Time* magazine that the two countries "have a common desire to accomplish the transition in a seamless way so that the users don't even notice it."[17]

The canal remains the single most important segment of Panama's economy, bringing in a full 20 percent of the nation's income. Despite all the questions and concerns swirling around Panama's imminent takeover of the canal, that reason alone is the canal's "saving grace," in General Nutting's view. "I believe they'll do what they have to do to keep the canal running,"[18] he says.

Chapter Two

BUILDING A CANAL

Oh, ye of little faith! Hear the words of M. de Lesseps, and believe![1]

> —printed in the French newspaper, *La Liberté*, in 1880, referring to Ferdinand de Lesseps' plan to build a Panama Canal

To comprehend the magnitude of what the United States accomplished in Panama is to understand the sacred place the canal occupies in American hearts. The building of the Panama Canal was a monumental feat. When it opened in 1914, the world touted it as the greatest engineering project in history. Many of the records set during its construction hold today, almost a century later. Contractors excavated 239 million cubic yards (182 million cubic m) of earth and rock to make way for the canal. Reporters of the time

Panama Canal locks, 1920s. The building of the canal was considered the greatest engineering feat in history.

noted that the amount of dirt extracted from Panama would fill railroad cars circling the globe four times.[2]

At the time the canal was built, the Gatun Dam, constructed to tame the Chagres River on the waterway's Atlantic side, was the largest such structure in the world. Gatun Lake, which the dam created, covered 163 square miles (422 sq km) and buried the homes of thousands of people. It was the largest man-made lake yet created.

Far more complicated than the Suez Canal, the "Big Ditch," as the Panama Canal came to be known, required the ingenuity and engineering genius of America's best minds. It also called upon the strength of legions of workers—most of whom came to Panama from the West Indies—and the determination of a people to see the job through. Perhaps most remarkable is the vision of those who designed the canal. They fashioned a waterway that would accommodate vessels almost 110 feet (33 m) wide and almost 1,000 feet (304 m) long, far larger than all but the biggest ships under construction in 1914, when the canal opened. Peering into the future, these master planners created a structure that would still meet the needs of commerce almost one hundred years hence.

MANY ROUTES

The tale of the Panama Canal—the structure that both bound and divided the United States and Panama—stretches back centuries and always revolves around gold. Indian guides led Spanish explorer Vasco Balboa across the isthmus to the Pacific Ocean in 1513. Soon after that discovery, adventurers in search of gold followed trails and rivers from the Caribbean/Atlantic side of the isthmus to the Pacific.

Later in the 1500s, Panama served as a base for Spanish conquistadors who stockpiled gold looted from native tribes there before shipping it to Spain. That brought pirates to Panama. In 1671, Welsh pirate Henry Morgan raided Panama City and burned it to the ground.

For the next two centuries, huge sailing ships from Europe followed the water route around the tip of Argentina to reach the Pacific. The discovery of gold in California in 1848 renewed interest in Panama as a shortcut from the Atlantic to the Pacific. Gold seekers wanting to avoid the treacherous trip across the Rocky Mountains instead headed for Panama, where the trail across the continent was a short 50 miles (80 m). They found the going tough, however, in the disease-infested jungles of Panama.

In 1850, New York entrepreneurs began construction of the world's first transcontinental railroad across the isthmus. By the time it was finished, in 1855, the railroad project had consumed $8 million, about $6.67 million over budget.[3] Nevertheless, the railroad profited, serving merchants and travelers passing between East and West.

The success of the railroad led to discussions of a canal that would allow shippers to travel from the Atlantic to the Pacific. A New York financier figured a Central American canal would save U.S. merchants $36 million a year in shipping costs.[4]

Where the canal should be built was unclear. Some argued for passage through Panama, a province of Colombia, along the Panama Railroad line. Panama, an isthmus in the shape of an **S** lying on its side, provided the shortest route, only 50 miles (80 km). But the route had problems: It passed through high mountains, which would require massive excavations for a canal. It also led into the jungle, where malaria, yellow fever, and other diseases thrived. At least six thousand workers—probably many more—had died during construction of the railroad.[5]

Others promoted a canal through Nicaragua. The route ran for 181 miles (291 km) from San Juan del Norte at the mouth of the San Juan River to Brito on the Pacific. Though longer than the Panama course, the Nicaraguan passage was quicker for Americans traveling from the East Coast to the West Coast because it was closer to the United States. It also had rivers and lakes that could be used in navigating the passage.

In 1848 Great Britain captured San Juan del Norte

CANAL ROUTES: Panama & Nicaragua

HONDURAS

NICARAGUA

Nicaragua Route

COSTA RICA

ATLANTIC OCEAN

CARIBBEAN SEA

Panama Route

PACIFIC OCEAN

PANAMA

COLOMBIA

and announced it planned to build a Nicaraguan canal. The United States opposed the project. It was a violation of the Monroe Doctrine, Americans said. The doctrine, issued by President James Monroe in 1823, stated the United States would not permit European nations to use armed force or take over new territory in the Western Hemisphere.

To avoid war, the United States and Great Britain signed the Clayton-Bulwer Treaty in 1850. In it, they agreed to share control over any canal built in Nicaragua. The two nations considered the treaty to cover canals built anywhere in Central America.

A third site for a possible canal ran across the Isthmus of Tehauntepec in northern Mexico, but it would have required 120 locks and twelve days to make the crossing.

Another proposal called for a canal running between Colombia and Panama. In all, about fourteen different routes were proposed at one time or another. It was a Frenchman who would finally settle on Panama.

"THE CANAL WILL BE MADE"

Ferdinand de Lesseps, known to all as "The Great Frenchman," was determined to build a canal across the isthmus of Panama. He had already succeeded in building a canal 100 miles (160 km) across the Egyptian desert at Suez. Proclaimed as a national hero, de Lesseps believed it would be easier to build a canal in Panama than it had been in Egypt. He formed a company, raised money, and set out to build a sea-level canal from Atlantic to Pacific. During a tour of Panama in 1879, de Lesseps followed almost every statement by the affirmation, "The canal will be made."[6]

Lieutenant Lucien Napoleon-Bonaparte Wyse, a grandson of Napoleon Bonaparte's brother Lucien, chose the canal route after surveying the area in 1877 and 1878. He rode on horseback for eleven days to reach Bogotá, the capital of Colombia. There he persuaded the president to sign an agreement granting de Lesseps' company the exclusive right to build a canal across Panama. In exchange, the company would pay Colombia a share of the income from the canal. The agreement, which was good for ninety-nine years, barred the company from selling its canal rights to a foreign country.

Work began in January 1881 with the arrival of the first team of French engineers. The plan promoted by de

Lesseps involved digging a trench from Colón on the Atlantic side of Panama to Panama City on the Pacific. Workers would have to slash their way through the jungle, dig through a 330-foot-high (100-m) mountain, and deal with the raging Chagres River.

To succeed, the engineers needed thousands of laborers. They turned to the West Indies, where people were eager to escape the poverty of their island homes. During the time the French worked on the canal, about fifty thousand black West Indians came to Panama seeking jobs.[7] The best workers earned up to $1.50 a day, a far better wage than any back home.[8]

Before they were done, the workers would dig out more than 78 million cubic yards (60 million cubic m) of soil and rock from the earth.[9] They used the latest equipment—locomotives, railroad cars, tugboats, dredging equipment, cranes, and steam shovels. They built more than two thousand buildings—houses for engineers and laborers, hospital facilities, offices, and machine shops.

But the French soon discovered the building of a canal in Panama was far more difficult than they had imagined. A few French engineers tried to convince de Lesseps to build a lock canal. With locks, they argued, workers wouldn't have to dig all the way through the mountain at Culebra Cut. The locks would lift ships up the mountain, then down to the sea. As it was, landslides filled in excavations in the mountain that had taken weeks to dig. De Lesseps, unconvinced, stuck to his original plan.

Problems with machinery also plagued the French. A dredging machine burned before it had begun work.

Culebra Cut

Delays and extra expenses, including $20 million to buy the Panama Railroad, threatened the company with financial disaster. And worst of all, laborers, engineers, and their families began dying by the thousands, struck down by yellow fever and malaria.

The French didn't know mosquitoes carry malaria and yellow fever from one victim to another. They had no screens to block the insects from entering the hospital, homes, and offices. Around the legs of the hospital beds and the trees outside, they placed buckets of water to keep away ants. The pools of water became breeding grounds for mosquitoes.

COST TOO HIGH

Finally, the French engineers convinced de Lesseps to build a lock system instead of a sea-level canal. But it was too late. The project had taken too long and cost too much. Stockholders refused to give the company more money. On May 15, 1889, the bankrupt company halted work on the canal. The entire effort cost $287 million. The cost in lives was far greater. An estimated twenty thousand workers died in Panama, most stricken with yellow fever or malaria. Some died in rock slides; others were the victims of dynamite blasts gone wrong.

De Lesseps died five years later at the age of 89, his mind cloudy and his dream to unite the Atlantic and the Pacific buried in the jungles of Panama.

ANCON HILL, 1890s

Almost all work stopped on the canal, workers returned to their island homes, and French engineers retreated to Europe. Traces of the monumental effort remained: dredges and other machinery, soon to be consumed by rust and jungle plants; buildings and machine shops, abandoned to the tropical weather.

Along a ledge carved into the side of the mountain, a collection of wooden buildings emerged amid tropical forests above and below. The cliff dropped precipitously into the valley; a retaining wall prevented strollers from tumbling down the steep incline. Here, at the hilltop l'Hôpital Nôtre Dame du Canal, French doctors and nuns had ministered to thousands of suffering workers. If one's imagination had ears, one could hear the groans of the men dying in this jungle hospital, suffering the last agonies of yellow fever and malaria. More men died of yellow fever in the hospital's second-story Ward Eleven, it is said, than in any other building in Panama.[10]

Chapter Three

AMERICANS TAKE OVER

They are doing something which will redound
immeasurably to the credit of America, which will benefit
all the world, and which will last for ages to come.[1]
                                    —Theodore Roosevelt
in a Special Message to Congress on the Panama Canal,
                                      December 17, 1906

When a gunman shot and killed President
William McKinley in 1901 and launched
Theodore Roosevelt into the presidency,
America was ripe for a canal. And Roosevelt, who had led
his men on a daring attack on Kettle Hill during the
Spanish American War, was now ready to charge into
Central America.

Americans had dreamed of a Central American canal
for more than half a century. An agreement signed with
Colombia (then known as New Grenada) in 1846 granted

Americans an exclusive right of way across its province of Panama. In exchange, the United States pledged to honor Colombia's sovereignty over the land. The United States also guaranteed the neutrality of the passageway "with the view that the free transit from the one to the other seas, may not be interrupted...while this Treaty exists."[2]

In the Clayton-Bulwer Treaty of 1850, Americans had worked out an understanding with Great Britain to build a Central American canal together. President Ulysses S. Grant had sent a survey team to the Isthmus of Darien in Panama and to Nicaragua in 1870 to find the best route. More surveys and reports followed while officials considered what course to follow.

The explosion of the U.S. battleship *Maine* off the coast of Cuba in February 1898 ignited Americans' desire for a canal. Americans blamed the Spanish for the explosion. They sided with Cuban rebels who wanted to be free of Spain's rule over the Caribbean island. Soon the two nations were at war.

The U.S. battleship *Oregon*, stationed in San Francisco, set sail for the Caribbean on March 19, 1898. Sixty-seven days later it arrived in Cuba. Those pushing for a canal pointed out that a passage across Central America would have cut the *Oregon*'s long journey short by almost a month.

In 1899 Congress allotted one million dollars for an Isthmian Canal Commission to conduct a final round of surveys on a canal site. Most Americans focused their attention on Nicaragua. The pass over the mountains was lowest there, and the country had a stable government

American engineers surveying Nicaragua

friendly to the United States, less disease, and a more suitable climate than Panama. The failure of the French in Panama made that site seem even less favorable. The commission recommended a Nicaraguan canal, though one engineer, George Morison, argued for Panama.

Only a few days before the commission's report became known, on November 18, 1901, the United States and Great Britain signed the Hay-Pauncefort Treaty. The new pact canceled the agreement in the Clayton-Bulwer Treaty for a joint canal and gave the United States exclusive rights to construct, regulate, and manage a waterway between the Atlantic and Pacific oceans. The Central American canal would be strictly an American affair.

THE BATTLE OF THE ROUTES

Two things happened next that would settle "The Battle of the Routes," the name given the dispute between those who favored a Panama Canal and those who wanted one in Nicaragua.

The French Panama Canal Company offered to sell its interests in the Panama Canal to the United States for $40 million. It was an offer worth considering. For its money, the United States would get an amazing array of ditch-digging equipment, railroad cars, two thousand or more buildings, the Panama Railroad, and all French rights to the crucial strip of land that crossed the isthmus. In addition, laborers working for the French had already dug up millions of cubic yards of earth along the canal route.

Behind the offer was a French engineer named Philippe Bunau-Varilla. Bunau-Varilla held stock in the French Panama Canal Company and had worked with de Lesseps in Panama. He was determined to finish the project his countrymen had begun.

With such an offer on the table, the U.S. canal commission took a second look at its report. Engineer Morison's arguments for Panama coupled with the French offer persuaded the commission members to change their views. They sent a new report favoring Panama to Congress. The commission's conclusions and the prospect of a good deal swayed President Roosevelt. He began to rally support for the Panama Canal.

Senator Marcus Hanna led the fight for Panama in the Senate. Supporters of the Nicaraguan canal waged a fierce battle for their site. In the end, though, Congress passed the Spooner Act giving Roosevelt the go-ahead to build a canal in Panama. The bill was named after its sponsor, Senator John C. Spooner.

In the closing days of argument on the Spooner Act,

Mount Pelée erupted in Martinique, an island in the West Indies, destroying the city of St. Pierre. Bunau-Varilla, eager to salvage the Panama project, spread the word that active volcanoes in Nicaragua would jeopardize any canal there. As luck would have it, Mount Momotombo erupted in Nicaragua a week later, but a cable supposedly from the nation's foreign minister denied the eruption had occurred. To prove his point, Bunau-Varilla sent each congressman a Nicaraguan stamp decorated with a spewing volcano. Below the stamp he wrote, "An official witness of the volcanic activity of Nicaragua."[3]

Some believe the action saved the Panama Canal. The Spooner Act passed by a vote of 67 to 6 in the Senate on June 19, 1902, and by a vote of 259 to 8 in the House. Roosevelt signed the bill into law on June 28, 1902. It authorized the president to buy the Panama rights and property from the French company for $40 million and to negotiate a treaty with Colombia to control a 6-mile (9.6-km) strip of land across the isthmus. If the deal with either the French or the Colombians couldn't be closed "within a reasonable time and upon reasonable terms,"[4] the president was to switch the canal site to Nicaragua.

REVOLUTIONARY SOLUTION

A delighted Roosevelt set out to fulfill the Spooner Act's instructions. Colombia, in the midst of a civil war, had watched the Senate action closely. The country desperately needed the money and economic development a U.S. canal would bring. Two Colombian negotiators tried and failed to work out an acceptable treaty with the

United States. U.S. Secretary of State John Hay warned a third diplomat, Dr. Tomás Herrán, that further delays would mean a Nicaraguan canal. Herrán reluctantly agreed to the pact proposed by Hay.

The Hay-Herrán Treaty, signed in Washington, D.C., on January 22, 1903, approved the transfer of French rights in Panama to the United States. For a fee of $10 million and annual payments of $250,000, Colombia gave the United States the exclusive right to build a canal across the strip that ran through Panama. The treaty, good for one hundred years, reaffirmed Colombia's sovereignty over the land.

When the treaty came before the U.S. Senate the following March, the legislators approved it by an overwhelming 73 to 5 vote. Colombian leaders, however, were faced with a dilemma. If they agreed to the pact, they feared the United States would try to take over sovereignty of the land, despite the guarantees in the treaty. If they held on to their rights as a nation, they would be forced to give up a "grand enterprise…that would surely result in a gigantic material improvement of our country."[5] On August 12, 1903, the Colombian Senate rejected the treaty.

An impatient Roosevelt wrote Hay his views on the matter in no uncertain terms: "I do not think that the Bogotá lot of jack rabbits should be allowed permanently to bar one of the future highways of civilization."[6]

Residents of Panama had watched the controversy with interest. They believed a canal in their territory would be a great benefit. Some wanted to make their own arrangements with the United States. They had already begun making secret plans to separate from Colombia and set up their own government.

Bunau-Varilla eagerly encouraged their efforts. He wanted a Panama Canal at all costs. An independent Panama, he believed, could be persuaded to accept a U.S. treaty. He offered the rebels money and support in exchange for a promise to appoint him foreign minister to the United States once Panama became a nation.

On November 2, 1903, the U.S.S. *Nashville* was sighted off Colón. The revolutionaries believed the ship's arrival was a signal of support from the United States. Bunau-Varilla had wired them as much, but there is no evidence the ship's crew or captain knew of the plot.[7]

Early the next morning, the crew of the Colombian gunboat *Cartagena* landed in Colón. A crafty American railroad official, James Shaler, persuaded the ship's officers to ride a railroad car to Panama City on the opposite coast. He pledged to transport the ship's crew later. Supporters of Panama's cause took the officers into custody when they arrived in Panama City. Soldiers in that city, who had been promised money in return for supporting the revolution, rallied around the rebels. As crowds cheered, the revolutionaries raised a new flag and proclaimed Panama a free nation.

Back in Colón, the commander of the *Nashville*, John Hubbard, ordered both sides not to use the railroad to transport troops. He took the action, he said, to protect the neutrality of the railroad line. When the officer left in charge of the Colombian troops heard of the uprising in Panama City, he threatened to kill all the Americans he could find. After a standoff between the Colombians and

American sailors from the *Nashville*, both sides retreated. The appearance of another U.S. ship, the *Dixie*, the next day, convinced the Colombians to return to Bogotá. Panamanians had told them that thousands of U.S. troops were headed for the isthmus, which was not true. The rebels paid the Colombians $8,000 to go home.[8]

A two-column article the next day on the front page of the *New York Times* reported Panama's secession from Colombia. "A Republic Is Declared" read the headline. A smaller headline informed readers: "The *Nashville* at Colón—Revolt Caused By Defeat of Canal Treaty— Annexation to United States May Be Object."[9]

CANAL TREATY RATIFIED

The role the United States played in Panama's revolution has been debated ever since. Roosevelt denied any direct involvement, though he did little to conceal his joy over the turn of events. The United States recognized the young nation on November 6. Colombia, of course, was furious. But the government had neither the money nor the power to assert its control over Panama. Other Latin American countries sent their sympathies—but no guns—to Bogotá.

Almost immediately, Bunau-Varilla took office as Panama's foreign minister. He was eager to seal a deal on the canal between the United States and Panama. On November 17, 1903, he presented Secretary of State Hay with his version of the Panama Canal treaty. The new pact surprised Hay. It was much more favorable to the United States than the Colombia treaty had been.

As in the previous pact, the Hay-Bunau-Varilla Treaty granted the United States the right to build the canal across Panama and guaranteed that the waterway would remain neutral. It awarded Panama a payment of $10 million outright and $250,000 annually. But instead of a one-hundred-year lease, the treaty granted Americans "the use, occupation and control" of a strip of land 10 miles (16 km) wide—instead of 6 miles (9.6 km)—"in perpetuity."[10] The agreement also gave the United States "all the rights, power and authority" over the zone as if it were "the sovereign of the territory."[11] The zone would be Panama's in name only. In reality, it would become the territory of the United States of America forever.

In return, the United States pledged to ensure Panama's newfound independence. It also agreed to take action to maintain the "public order" in Panama City and Colón. In a rush to approve the document before Panama's new leaders objected, Bunau-Varilla and Hay signed the treaty November 18, 1903, at Hay's home.

As expected, the new terms angered the Panamanians. But convinced by Bunau-Varilla that the treaty would benefit Panama, they agreed to ratify it. In an elaborate ceremony in Panama City on December 3, the leaders of Panama opened the iron box Bunau-Varilla had sent. Inside, wrapped in the flag of Panama, the treaty awaited their signatures. After signing the document with a special gold pen, they sent it back to Washington, wrapped in the flags of both nations.[12] The U.S. Senate ratified the pact in short order on February 23, 1904, and Roosevelt signed the ratification bill the next day.

On May 2, 1904, the new Republic of Panama

received its first installment of a $10 million payment from the United States. A week later, the United States paid the French Panama Canal Company $40 million. At the time, the payment was the largest real estate transaction on record.[13] The United States later paid Colombia $25 million for its claims to Panama.

WAR ON MOSQUITOES

On May 4, 1904, Lieutenant Mark Brooke raised the stars and stripes over the old Grand Hotel, where the French canal company had had its offices. It was a quiet start for a momentous project.

Soon, however, American builders and West Indian laborers would fill the air with the booming of earthdiggers and the blast of dynamite. The seven-man team supervising canal construction selected John Wallace, a U.S. railroad engineer, as chief engineer of the project. General George W. Davis would serve as governor of the Canal Zone. Dr. William Crawford Gorgas, an Army doctor who was an expert in tropical diseases, accompanied the group to Panama.

The first order of business was cleaning the area around the canal route. Engineers designed sewers and provided clean, running water to Panama City and Colón. An outbreak of yellow fever in the spring and summer of 1905 caused a panic among workers. Taking a lesson from the French disaster, Americans determined to keep their workforce healthy. Preventing yellow fever and malaria became as important to the success of the mission as the construction work.

By the early 1900s, scientists knew that mosquitoes spread the diseases. With support from John Stevens, who replaced Wallace as chief engineer in June 1905, Gorgas supervised a work crew of four thousand men to rid the area of mosquitoes. From his base at Ancon Hospital, Gorgas ordered every house in Panama City sprayed. He drained pools of water, where the mosquitoes bred. Screens were put in all windows, and grass and weeds were trimmed. The doctor spent $90,000 on screens alone.[14] By December, yellow fever had been eradicated in the Canal Zone.

Gorgas waged a successful campaign against malaria as well. Death by pneumonia, typhoid fever, and other causes dipped dramatically. By the time the canal was finished, the death rate of Canal Zone residents had dropped below that in the United States. Only 414 workers died in 1913–1914, compared with 1,273 in 1907–1908.[15] Black workers, however, fared worse than U.S. employees. Their death rate for the final year was 8.23 per thousand, while the rate for whites was 2.06 per thousand.[16] Both blacks and whites, however, benefited from the steps Gorgas took to prevent disease. During the ten years of the U.S. canal project, approximately 5,600 canal workers died of disease and accidents.[17] Almost four times as many people died while working on the French canal.

BATTLE OF THE LEVELS

Congress had never decided what kind of a canal should be built in Panama. Most people thought a system of locks would work best. But chief engineer Wallace began to promote a sea-level canal. He believed a trench through the isthmus would be simpler and cheaper than mechanical locks.

When Stevens replaced Wallace, he, too, supported a sea-level design. Once in Panama, however, he realized the powerful Chagres River would destroy a sea-level canal. He turned to the lock system. A huge dam would have to be built to control the river. The river water would be used to form a lake at the highest point in the canal. Water, slowly drained from the lake, would be used to raise ships in the locks. A lock canal would also reduce the amount of digging at Culebra Cut, where the continental divide ran through the canal route.

Those who favored a sea-level canal fought for Congressional approval. But Stevens persuaded the lawmakers to support a lock system. He won "The Battle of the Levels" on a slim 36 to 31 vote in the Senate. The House also approved the measure, which specified that a dam, locks, and a lake be built in Panama. Roosevelt signed the bill on June 29, 1906.

WORLD'S GREATEST ENGINEERING FEAT

Now that the design had been approved, Stevens set to work. Organizing the project became a monumental task. Like the French, the Americans turned to the West Indies for cheap labor. But they also hired people from around the world who came to Panama seeking jobs. About 250,000 workers participated in the project over the decade it took Americans to build the canal.

Stevens used railroad cars traveling along tracks to transport dirt removed from the trenches. Teams of men shifted the tracks of the railroad line as the work progressed. It was a common-sense way of moving earth, but no one had thought of it before. The system saved a tremendous amount of time. The fill was used to build the monstrous dam along the Chagras River.

President Roosevelt visited the construction site in November 1906. It was the first time a U.S. president had been outside the country during his term of office. The playful Roosevelt posed in a massive, 95-ton steam shovel, working the controls and asking endless questions about its operation.

The work was hard and dangerous. Smoke, dust, and dirt filled the air. The temperature during the day rose to 100°F (37.8°C). Steam shovel operators worked side by side in the cut, dumping their loads into waiting railroad cars. Men drilled into rock. Dynamite sticks were buried into the hillside and ignited. If the charge wasn't set right or if a spark hit the sticks, a blast could kill all those standing nearby. The noise at the site was overwhelming.

John Stevens resigned in February 1907, and George W. Goethals, an Army colonel, took his place. Goethals took charge immediately. Stevens had set the stage. Now it was up to Goethals to complete the task. In the next seven years, Goethals encountered massive problems. The biggest challenge was Culebra Cut, where workers dug a trench through the continental divide. Beginning in January 1907, workers excavated more than 500,000 cubic yards (381,679 cubic m) a month from Culebra Cut. In March 1912—the busiest month of the project—

Roosevelt at the controls at the Panama Canal, 1906

3,217 trains with 65,555 railroad cars carried dirt out of the big hole.[18]

All along the 9 miles (14.4 km) of the cut, steam shovels and dynamite crews tore chunks of earth from the mountain. Huge sections repeatedly slid from the top of the cut into the ditch already cleared. The landmark was later named Gaillard Cut in honor of David Gaillard, the engineer who supervised the operation there.

By summer 1914, the canal was almost complete. Workers had built the most massive dam and the greatest man-made lake the world had ever seen. They had spent four years assembling the world's highest locks—three pairs of them. The lock gates were enormous, 7 feet (2.1 m) thick and weighing up to 770 tons each. The gates at the Miraflores Locks were the tallest ever built. Some 80 feet (24 m) high, they prevented the 20-foot-high (6-m) tides on the Pacific side from disrupting the water level of the locks. The gates were so well designed that they required no more than a 25-horsepower motor to open them.

The canal project cost the United States $352 million. Remarkably, builders completed the project on time and for $23 million less than had been projected in 1907.[19]

Thousands of workers played a vital role in creating the Panama Canal. But no one has a stronger link to the canal than Theodore Roosevelt. For years afterward, Roosevelt defended his role as a man of action in the Panama Canal affair. During a speech at the University of California in 1911, he told students:

> The Panama Canal would not have been started if I had not taken hold of it, because if I had followed the traditional or conservative method I should have submitted an admirable state paper occupying a couple of hundred pages...there would have been a number of excellent speeches...the debate would be proceeding at this moment with great spirit and the beginning of work on the canal would be fifty years in the future.[20]

Chapter Four

SIMMERING CONFLICTS

By creating a small community of licensed haves,...
the Zone created a larger one of have-nots. Across a
fenceless, invisible but palpable boundary, Panamanians
watched like urchins with their faces pressed against a
restaurant window, aware that if they were fortunate,
they might be admitted, to some degree, to this
privileged body by accepting a low job.[1]

—Carl Posey, former Zonian

he steamship *Ancon* sailed through the new
ocean highway on August 15, 1914, officially
opening the canal amid banners, cheers, and
speeches. Dignitaries crowded the deck as the U.S. Navy
ship made the transit in record time—nine hours.
Goethals, watching from the locks at Balboa, pronounced
he was "manifestly pleased" at the crossing.[2]

Flags of all nations flew from the ship's masts, with the
Panamanian flag prominently displayed at the front of

the vessel and the U.S. stars and stripes on the jackstaff. The flag of the American Peace Society flew from the foremast, but the *New York Times* reporter describing the scene ironically noted that below decks "two huge pieces of artillery" stood ready to defend the waterway. World War I had just erupted in Europe, and the United States wanted to guard against an enemy attack on the canal.

"The Panama Canal is open to the commerce of the world,"[3] the *New York Times* announced on its front page the next day. Four cargo ships and a yacht waited to cross the canal after the festivities.

Americans burst with pride at the achievement. A New York man, anticipating the grand opening, proposed in a letter to the *New York Times* published July 16, 1914, that another star be added to the U.S. flag to commemorate the Canal Zone.[4]

While the proposal failed to win adoption, people in the United States viewed the canal as a symbol of American ingenuity. "A stupendous undertaking," Secretary of War Lindley Garrison called it, "a perpetual memorial to the genius and enterprise of our people."[5]

MIXED FEELINGS

Panamanians were among the two thousand people who stood on the shores and cheered. But they greeted the completion of the great project with mixed feelings. The effort to build the Panama Canal had resulted in the birth of their nation. It had provided jobs and boosted the economy of their country. The United States had practically rid the area of malaria and yellow fever.

Panama's cities had paved streets, sewers, running water, and electricity.

Now that the project was done, however, Panama had to pay a price for the benefits it received from the canal. Hundreds of unemployed immigrants—who shared neither the culture nor the language of their host country—crowded the slums of the cities along the Canal Zone. Under the terms of the 1903 treaty, Americans had the right "in perpetuity" to run the most lucrative business in Panama—the canal. The best jobs at the canal would go to Americans. Only a few Panamanians would be allowed into the upper levels of Canal Zone society. Some would compete with West Indian workers for jobs that required unskilled labor. Most Panamanians would live outside the Canal Zone, working in low-paying jobs in the cities or farming in the rural areas.

The treaty also gave the United States the right to control a 10-mile-wide (16-km) strip running through Panama. Panamanians living and working there would be forced to abide by U.S. laws. Most, however, would be barred from the protected world that thrived inside the borders of the zone.

All these conditions produced tensions between Panama and the United States. Through the years, conflicts simmered and occasionally flared until, in the 1960s, they threatened to ignite into violent confrontations.

INSIDE THE ZONE

From the beginning, the U.S. Army controlled the Canal Zone. The Secretary of the Army was the sole stock-

holder of the Panama Canal Company, which administered the canal. Working under the canal company, the
Army Civil Works Division, a branch of the Army, supervised the day-to-day operation of the canal. The Army's
Southern Command was in charge of defending the
canal and overseeing life in the zone. U.S. courts meted
out justice; U.S. laws regulated everyday life. American
flags flew over the canal and buildings that housed U.S.
government offices and U.S. schools.

Zone society was divided into two separate universes.
U.S. citizens called Zonians, who held the skilled, professional jobs, were termed gold workers. Unskilled laborers,
mostly black West Indians and a few Panamanians, were
silver workers. The terms dated back to the days when
canal construction workers were paid in silver, and engineers and other U.S. professionals received their wages in
more-valuable gold bullion.

As described in the Panama Canal employment policy, gold employees were those who worked in the "skilled
trades and in the executive, supervisory, professional,
sub-professional, clerical and other positions where education, training, and special qualifications are required."[6]
They received the same pay workers in comparable jobs
in the United States earned, plus a 25 percent bonus for
working outside the country. Inevitably, the top jobs were
filled by U.S. citizens, though some Panamanians who
had political ties or came from wealthy families and a few
Europeans held gold jobs as well.

Silver employees worked as laborers, performing
work "that does not require the services of highly trained
or qualified persons." Such positions were reserved for

50

Clubhouse at Balboa in the Canal Zone

"those natives of the tropics, a considerable number of whom are Panamanians."[7]

The two groups were strictly separated. In addition to higher pay, the gold workers lived in rent-free homes built, owned, and maintained by the U.S. government. Most silver workers lived in cheap, overcrowded tenements in Panama City or Colón. Those who lived in the Canal Zone had to pay rent, a situation that continued until 1951.[8] The U.S. government provided medical facilities, schools, and bonuses to U.S. gold workers. Government buildings and offices had separate facilities for gold and silver workers. Black children attended crowded, underfunded schools that offered classes only through the ninth grade. Even water fountains were marked "gold" and "silver."

Originally the system had been set up to reward enterprising workers. Employees—both black and white—in the silver ranks could be promoted to the gold category by working hard and becoming skilled at their jobs. By 1908, however, the rolls served as a way of separating black from white workers.

Carl Posey, who grew up in the Canal Zone in the 1950s and 1960s and whose father was an American engineer, describes a hometown seemingly plucked from Middle America and deposited in the tropics of Panama. Isolated from their host nation by an invisible barrier, zone residents could as well have been living in Kansas. Wide, well-paved streets ran past freshly painted houses with manicured lawns, close-cropped grass, and screened windows. At the commissary—army stores open only to zone residents—one could buy a Coke and American comic books, maple syrup, and U.S. postage stamps. It was an odd sort of existence, living in pristine government housing on a twisting piece of land where the sun rose from the Pacific Ocean, a rather bizarre sight for those used to seeing the Pacific on the western horizon.

GRIEVANCES

From the early days of the Canal Zone, silver workers had sought fairer treatment. A labor delegation representing West Indian workers presented U.S. Secretary of War D. Newton Baker with a list of grievances in December 1919. Baker promised to discuss the workers' complaints with the canal government. The workers and the canal administrators held several conferences on the matter. Finally, in 1920, the two sides forged a fourteen-point agreement, which they presented to Governor Chester Harding. His response was unequivocal:

"I will not enter into an agreement, written or otherwise, with a committee of employees concerning rates of pay or conditions of employment."[9]

Such matters, the governor contended, could be set only by administrative order. In other words, it was up to him and not the workers what the pay and conditions would be. The angry workers called a strike. In retaliation, Harding fired all those who did not return to work. The union and the labor organizations that followed were forced to sign a pledge that their members would never go out on strike again.

West Indian carpenters pose outside a manager's house under construction in the Canal Zone

The Americans who ran the canal generally preferred to hire West Indian workers. The West Indians spoke English, and many had been previously trained by U.S. supervisors during the first days of canal construction. They could also be separated by race from white American workers. White Panamanian workers would object to being segregated from other whites and that would lead to the breakdown of the system, canal officials feared.[10]

While U.S. officials controlled the Canal Zone, Panamanian dictators ruled the country. The national police force—Guardia Nacional (National Guard)—ensured that the ruling party stayed in power. Backed by the United States, the dictators passed laws that favored American business and sold rights to their country's lands and resources. Since the mid-1800s, the United States had sent in troops whenever Latin Americans threatened American businesses or property.

In 1918, Panamanians protested when American oil companies took over land in the province of Chiriquí, to the west of the Canal Zone. After a few violent clashes, U.S. troops moved into the province and stayed for two years. When Costa Rica and Panama threatened war over disputed land along their boundary in 1921, U.S. Marines again landed in Panama. The troops forced Panama to turn the land over to Costa Rica. Marines marched into Panama a third time in 1925 when mobs threatened to take over Panama City during a rent strike. The 1903 treaty gave the United States the right to "maintain public order" in the cities along the Canal Zone. But Panamanians fiercely resented U.S. involvement in their affairs.

Good Neighbor Policy

In 1933 U.S. President Franklin D. Roosevelt introduced his Good Neighbor policy. He hoped to improve relations with the nations to the south. Pledging not to interfere with Latin American internal affairs, he offered to help the countries build roads, improve public health, and strengthen their economies. He also removed U.S. Marines from nearby Nicaragua, where they had been stationed since 1926 to protect U.S. businesses.

In 1935, Panama diplomat Ricardo Alfaro began to push for a new U.S.-Panama treaty. Signed in 1936, the Hull-Alfaro treaty granted few concessions to Panama. Among the benefits it conferred was an increase in Panama's annual canal payment from $250,000 to $430,000. It also eliminated Panama's status as a protectorate of the United States, turning over responsibility for maintaining Panama's independence to Panama. In addition, Panama—not the United States—would now be responsible for maintaining order in Panama City, Colón, and the lands nearby.

The treaty eliminated a provision that had allowed the United States to take property by eminent domain in Panama City and Colón for canal use. Under the new terms, the United States would have to gain Panama's permission before taking property for the canal. The treaty continued America's control of the canal and the Canal Zone in perpetuity, as agreed to in the 1903 treaty. After lengthy debate, the U.S. Senate ratified the treaty in 1939. That same year Panama's president ratified the pact for his country.

With the increase of world trade after the Great Depression, Panama's economy, bolstered by the canal, boomed. The Panama Canal Company encouraged West Indians to move to Panama to fill new jobs. The arrival of thousands of West Indians roused the resentment of native Panamanians. A new Panamanian constitution passed in 1941 denied citizenship to all residents born after 1928 whose parents weren't legal citizens of Panama. Most of those affected by the new law were black West Indians whose parents had migrated to Panama years before to work on the canal. Many of these young people considered themselves Panamanians. They had been born in Panama, spoke Spanish, and followed the customs of their neighbors. They began to agitate for better treatment in their adopted homeland.

In 1944, leading Panamanians—Hispanic as well as West Indian—called for a new constitution that avoided racial discrimination. Under pressure from popular leader Pancho Arias, Panama's president, Ricardo Adolfo de la Guardia, annulled the 1941 constitution. He also granted citizenship to those who had lost it when the constitution went into effect. These new citizens would lead the battle to improve conditions among the non-U.S. Canal Zone workers.

During World War II, the United States stationed seventy thousand troops in Panama to protect the canal. Without the vital waterway, U.S. Navy ships would have had great difficulty fighting enemies on both the European and Asian fronts. Once the war ended, the United States wanted to keep troops at bases in Panama. In a pact signed in December 1947, Panama's foreign minister agreed to allow U.S. troops to remain in the country. Angered by the decision, Panamanians rioted, and the National Assembly rejected the agreement.

SEEKING FAIR TREATMENT

The treatment of local workers at the Canal Zone led to more unrest. Some U.S. officials worried that the blatantly unequal treatment of Panamanians would push dissatisfied workers into supporting the Communists, who had increased activities in Latin America since World War II. Other Americans called for better treatment of the Panamanian Canal Zone laborers as the moral thing to do. They believed the United States would strengthen its position in the world by improving relations with Panama.

The U.S. Army was the first to take steps to eliminate segregation among the workforce in the Canal Zone. From 1946 to 1954, the army desegregated its bases and opened facilities and clubhouses to members of both races. Civil employees continued to be paid based on their race, however, with U.S. workers receiving higher wages than their Panamanian coworkers.

Private contractors and canal officials resisted any move to desegregate the Canal Zone. General J. C. Mehaffey, governor of the Canal Zone at the time, claimed that the area couldn't be desegregated "without wrecking the Panama Canal." White workers would quit, he warned, and those who stayed would be less inclined to work hard. He did agree to take down the offensive "gold" and "silver" signs posted on public buildings. The terms were changed to "U.S. rate" and "local-rate" in 1948, but unequal wages for the two groups remained intact.[11]

In the late 1940s, the Congress of Industrial Organizations took over the work of the Panama Canal West Indian Employees Association, which had represented black workers since the early days of the Canal Zone. Union officials recruited Hispanic Panamanians as well as blacks in their battle for workers' rights. By joining forces, they hoped to have more power in their fight against the discriminatory Canal Zone wage system.

By 1949, the local Panamanian newspaper was hopeful enough to publish an editorial foreseeing "a new day," when Panamanian workers would no longer have to endure "the prescriptive wage policies and discriminatory practices that caused non-U.S. citizens of the Federal Government to earn salaries on the basis of their nationality, and live under social conditions determined by the hue of their skin."[12]

NEW TREATY

In 1952, newly elected Panamanian President José Remón demanded better treatment for canal workers and more money from canal tolls. A crowd of one hundred thousand people cheered Remón at a rally as he prepared to meet with U.S. officials to seek changes in the U.S.-Panama treaty.

The new treaty, signed in 1955, granted Panama some concessions, although it left untouched the clause guaranteeing America's right to control the canal and the Canal Zone "in perpetuity." The pact boosted Panama's

The Bridge of the Americas built in 1960 connected for the first time the two halves of Panama split by the canal.

annual canal payments to $1,930,000. It also guaranteed that Panamanian canal workers would receive wages, benefits, and job opportunities equal to those of their American coworkers. To comply with the treaty, Congress passed a law in 1958 that set up one pay scale for all workers at the Canal Zone and banned discrimination against workers because of race or national origin. The gap between wages paid Panamanians and those U.S. workers received would remain for almost two more decades, however.

The new treaty provisions also required that the United States build a bridge spanning the canal. The $20 million bridge, completed in 1960, for the first time connected the two halves of Panama divided by the canal for more than half a century.

SCHOOL RULING

Another U.S. action against racism—this time in the courts—would have a major impact on Panama. In 1954 the U.S. Supreme Court, ruling in the landmark case *Brown* v. *Board of Education,* ordered the desegregation of the nation's schools. The ruling applied to U.S. military bases and the Canal Zone. Canal Zone officials quickly converted the black schools, which had been English-speaking, to Spanish-speaking Panamanian schools. The officials said they made the move to save money, but others suggested a more sinister motive: The conversion allowed authorities to avoid the order to desegregate the canal schools.[13] The converted schools, however, served to connect the black students more solidly to their homeland, teaching them Spanish, Panamanian history, and local culture.

While relations between black and Hispanic Panamanians improved, relations between Panamanians and the American officials who ruled the Canal Zone deteriorated. A population boom after World War II had put huge demands on Panama. The country could not provide enough housing, schools, and social services for its people. Inside the Canal Zone, however, Americans continued to live in relative luxury. For years the United Fruit Company and other U.S. firms controlled the Panamanian economy. U.S. commissaries inside the Canal Zone sold items to canal workers at low prices. This cut into the business of Panamanian shops and deprived Panama of taxes on the goods.

On the political front, factions battled for power. Remón was murdered in 1955 and was replaced by Vice-President Ricardo Arias, the son of Pancho Arias.

Chapter Five

RALLYING AROUND THE FLAG

The United States is a nation drunk with power;
Panama's cause is the cause of all the Americas.[1]
    —Miguel Moreno Jr., Panama's Ambassador
     to the Organization of American States
         January 1964

In this atmosphere of poverty, instability, and resentment, the flags of Panama and the United States became flashpoints. The stars and stripes had flown over the Canal Zone since the days of the 1903 treaty that gave the United States power over the canal and its surrounding land. To Americans working in the Canal Zone, their flag symbolized the pride they felt in being part of such a massive undertaking as the Panama Canal, the "Eighth Wonder of the World."

To Panamanians, however, the American flag was a constant reminder of Panama's subservient position in relation to the "Colossus of the North." The United States—not Panama—controlled the nation's most valuable resource, its canal.

Panamanian students entered the Canal Zone several times in the 1950s to protest the fact that the American flag, rather than the flag of their own country, flew over the canal. In 1959, protesters tore down the U.S. flag flying in front of the American embassy and stoned U.S. agency buildings. They rioted after U.S. soldiers prevented them from entering the Canal Zone. The leaders of the protest demanded the United States split proceeds from the canal equally with Panama.

Americans watched the growing unrest in Panama with alarm. Many in the United States feared Panamanians would turn to the Communists if their demands for better treatment were not met. President Dwight Eisenhower proposed a nine-point plan that, among other things, called for raises for the lowest-level canal workers, more job opportunities for Panamanians, and better housing for local Canal Zone workers. Housing units were built, but canal authorities, as they had done for decades, resisted labor and wage reforms.

ALLIANCE FOR PROGRESS

Soon after his inauguration in 1961, U.S. President John F. Kennedy announced the Alliance for Progress. The ten-year, $20 billion plan was designed to help Latin American nations with economic development, land reform, and financial stability. By the end of 1964, the United States had spent $3.5 billion on the program and had pledged \$4.2 billion.[2] Kennedy, like Eisenhower, pushed canal authorities to upgrade labor relations in the Canal Zone. Despite pressure from Washington, wages and job opportunities for Panamanians lagged far behind those of their American counterparts. In 1961, only 240 Panamanians worked at jobs paying the U.S. rate, which was four times higher than the rate paid local workers.[3]

The inequities fed hostilities between the United States and Panama. The treaty provision granting U.S. control over the Panama Canal Zone "in perpetuity" remained in force and continued to rankle Panamanians. Speaking before the United Nations General Assembly in late 1962, Panama's foreign minister, Galileo Solis, described the treaty as "humiliating, injurious, unjust and inequitable."[4]

Emotional disputes over the two countries' flags continued to erupt. To ease tensions, the United States in January 1963 agreed to fly the flags of both countries as an acknowledgment of Panama's role in the canal. The agreement did little, however, to address the underlying problems that separated the two nations. In a year's time, the dispute would explode onto the front pages of the world's newspapers.

FLAG FUROR

On Tuesday, January 7, 1964, several hundred American students marched to the flagpole in front of Balboa High School in the Panama Canal Zone. Solemnly, they unfurled the U.S. flag they carried and hoisted it up the pole. The action violated an order issued earlier in the school year by the governor of the Canal Zone. A 1963 order required that the flags of both the United States and Panama be flown jointly throughout the Canal Zone. When U.S. parents objected to having the Panama flag fly at their children's schools, the governor decreed that no flags would be flown in front of U.S. schools in the zone.

Canal Zone officials quickly took the flag down. After they left, students raised it once more. The story of their actions soon spread to other American schools in the zone. On Wednesday, students at several schools raised their own American flags. They signed petitions to U.S. President Lyndon Johnson to allow them to fly the flag at their schools.

The students' act of defiance did not go unnoticed in Panama. On Thursday, January 9, Panamanian students in nearby Panama City marched to Balboa High School, where American students were milling around the flagpole. Five Panamanian students carried their nation's red, white, and blue flag to the flagpole and planted it beside the U.S. flag. Canal Zone police at the scene protected them from harm.

Ordered by the police to return to Panama City, the group of students marched back to the capital. Along the way, angry students shattered the glass in a few street lights and overturned garbage cans.

PANAMANIANS ENRAGED

The incident enraged Panamanians. Told and retold, the students' tale spread throughout towns and cities all along the Canal Zone. According to one account, a Pana-

Panamanian high school students and Canal Zone police clash over a torn Panamanian flag. The dispute over flags sparked a riot that claimed the lives of 24 people.

manian flag had been torn down and trampled. As darkness fell, thousands of angry protesters gathered along the streets that divided Panama from the Canal Zone. In Panama City, they surged across John F. Kennedy Avenue, once known as Fourth of July Avenue before it was renamed in honor of the late U.S. president.

Overwhelming the police force, the mob overturned cars, burned buildings, smashed windows, and threw stones at officers standing in their way. Flames consumed a laundry and U.S. District Judge Guthrie F. Crowe's house. Canal Zone police used baseball bats, tear gas, and shock grenades (weapons designed to stun people but not kill them) to repel the angry protesters. Some officers fired shots into the crowd.

In Colón, 38 (61 km) miles northwest of Panama City, ten thousand demonstrators planted a Panamanian flag in the Canal Zone and stoned the U.S. consulate building. Unable to control the mobs, the police called the army for help. Arriving in tanks and armored cars, the army soon forced the Panamanians back across the street. By 11 P.M., the protesters had left the Canal Zone. But the violence didn't end there. For the next three days, mobs rioted in the streets of Panama City and Colón. Finally, Panama's National Guard posted armed officers throughout the cities. On January 13, the streets were peaceful at last.

Twenty-four people—twenty Panamanians and four Americans—died in the violence; two hundred were injured. Damage to buildings and property was estimated at more than $2 million. The offices of several American-owned companies, as well as government buildings, were destroyed. Panamanians, defiantly clinging to the righteousness of their cause, renamed John F. Kennedy Avenue, the street dividing the Canal Zone and Panama City, the Avenue of the Martyrs.

The flag riots brought to a head the disputes between the United States and Panama. Even before the rioting ended, Panamanian President Roberto Chiari suspended relations with the United States and filed a complaint with the Organization of American States against American aggression. He warned that if U.S. President Johnson did not agree to renegotiate the Panama Canal treaty, his

country would not resume diplomatic relations with the
United States.

PANAMA SEEKS CONTROL

Panama's leaders had long sought sovereignty over
the Canal Zone. They wanted the United States to
acknowledge that the Canal Zone was part of Panama
and to turn control of the region over to them. Panamanians also wanted more money for allowing the canal to
operate in Panama. But until now, most Panamanian
leaders had not called for the United States to turn over
control of the canal. In 1960, President Roberto Chiari
had told a reporter: "I do not seek the nationalization of
the Panama Canal by Panama. I am satisfied for the
United States to continue the operation of the Panama
Canal."[5]

In the wake of the flag riots, however, Chiari called for
"substantive changes" in the canal treaty.[6] U.S. President
Johnson made no promises, but he agreed to discuss the
issues. Panama renewed ties with the United States on
April 4, 1964, and negotiators for the two nations began
work on a new treaty.

TREATIES DRAFTED

By 1967, three treaties had been drafted and initialed
by both sides. But the treaties were never signed by President Johnson and Marcos Robles, who had succeeded
Chiari as president of Panama. The first treaty granted
Panama many of the concessions it had sought:

- A Panama Canal Commission, with nine Americans and Panamanians, would operate the canal.
- Most of the lands along the canal would be placed under Panama's control.
- Most businesses on the Canal Zone would be closed, to be replaced by Panamanian firms.
- Panama and the United States would operate the Canal Zone courts jointly.

President Lyndon Johnson agreed to negotiations for a new Panama Canal treaty after riots in Panama threatened United States–Central American relations.

- Applicants for canal jobs would be hired based on merit, not nationality.
- The two countries would share tolls collected by the canal.

A second treaty guaranteed that the canal would remain neutral and gave the United States permission to keep its military bases in Panama indefinitely. The third treaty gave the United States the right to build a sea-level canal without locks to allow bigger ships to pass through the canal and to speed up traffic. The joint commission would supervise the new canal, and the United States would have a say in canal management until the year 2067 if a new canal were built.

When the terms of the treaties were leaked to the press, groups in both countries reacted with outrage. Labor unions representing Panamanian canal workers opposed the treaties because they feared the changes would mean cuts in wages and benefits. As a result of hard-won battles by the unions, canal salaries were higher than those earned by Panamanians outside the Canal Zone. Panamanian leaders had suggested that the wages be lowered to create a fairer wage scale throughout the nation. "Some workers may suffer adversely in the changeover, but the interests of the nation must be considered above those of any special groups,"[7] Congresswoman Leonor Sullivan had told the *Panama Tribune*.

Other Panamanians, still seething over the flag riots, objected to any U.S. control. They wanted Panama to have sole power over the Canal Zone and the canal, and they wanted the U.S. military out of their country.

Americans were just as adamant in their demands to control the canal. Long-since enshrined as the best symbol of the can-do American spirit, the canal continued to hold a place of honor among U.S. citizens. They didn't want to give it up.

Panama's leaders wanted to avoid a debate on the issue before their upcoming elections. Likewise, Johnson, embroiled in the controversy over the Vietnam War, did not want to offend any more voters. The leaders tabled the treaties until after the elections. Three more U.S. presidents would serve before the Panama Canal treaties were finally settled.

Chapter Six

NEGOTIATING A NEW TREATY

The Panama Canal is a vast heroic expression of that
age-old desire to bridge a divide and to bring people
closer together. This is what the treaties are all about.[1]
—President Jimmy Carter

The treaty is like a little pebble which we shall be able to
carry in our shoe for twenty-three years. And that is
better than the stake we have had to carry in our hearts.[2]
—General Omar Torrijos

Arnulfo Arias won Panama's presidential election and was inaugurated on October 1,
1968. Eleven days later, Omar Torrijos, head
of the National Guard, led a junta that deposed Arias and
seized control of Panama. The Panama Canal treaties
stayed on hold while General Torrijos worked to make
Panama's government more efficient and less corrupt.
He included blacks in his government, banned political

parties, and sought support from the poor, Indians, students, and labor unions. Torrijos built roads, brought development to the nation's poor rural areas, and persuaded bankers from all over the world to establish an international banking center in Panama. Such accomplishments, coupled with his easy charm and rural roots, made him a popular figure among Panama's common people.

When a group of National Guard officers tried to depose Torrijos in December 1969, a young National Guard officer, Manuel Noriega, supported him and provided an army escort back to Panama City. Thousands of supporters accompanied Torrijos back to the capital to show their support. Barbara Melville, who with her husband, Robert, lived in Panama in the 1990s as a participant in the Episcopal Church's Volunteers for a Mission program, says Panamanians still revere Torrijos.[3]

TREATIES REJECTED

Panama formally rejected the three U.S.-Panama treaties in 1970. In June 1971, with the Panamanian people solidly behind him, Torrijos decided to resume treaty negotiations with the United States. This time, Panama demanded full sovereignty over the Canal Zone. The United States, with Richard Nixon now in the presidency, continued to call for joint rule over the territory. After six months, neither side had budged, and it looked as if the negotiations would fail again.

Demetrios Lakas was named president of Panama in 1972, but Torrijos continued to hold the reins of power.

Torrijos took his battle to the nations of the world. At his invitation, the United Nations' Security Council met in Panama on March 21, 1973. The Panamanian delegation introduced a resolution granting "full respect for Panama's effective sovereignty over all of its territory."[4] The measure won the support of all but two of the thirteen members of the Security Council. (Great Britain did not vote on the matter.) In a rare move, the United States vetoed the resolution, saying it did not take U.S. interests into account.

The episode turned world opinion against the United States, and brought almost all the nations of Latin America into Panama's camp. Panama's foreign minister, Juan Antonio Tack, summed up the reaction to the vote well when he said, "The United States vetoed the measure...but the rest of the world vetoed the United States."[5]

NEW NEGOTIATIONS

Under pressure from other nations to settle the canal question, President Nixon decided to tone down U.S. demands. With the Watergate scandal swirling around him, Nixon handed the canal matter to Secretary of State Henry Kissinger. Kissinger appointed Ellsworth Bunker, ambassador-at-large, to head the U.S. negotiating team.

At the time of his appointment, Bunker was 77 years old. He would be 83 by the time negotiations ended. A well-respected diplomat who had served as ambassador to Argentina, Italy, and India, Bunker had helped settle disputes in West New Guinea and Yemen. After President

Lyndon Johnson sent twenty-five thousand troops to the Dominican Republic in 1965 to stop Cuban forces from taking over, Bunker negotiated a peaceful—and face-saving—troop withdrawal. Johnson called on him again during the early stages of the Vietnam War. The president reportedly told Bunker, "I want you to go to Vietnam," he said. "It's the most important problem facing the country today, and I need you there."[6]

Bunker's job as chief U.S. negotiator on the canal treaty team was to preserve American interests in Panama while recognizing the needs of the Panamanians. It was no easy task. The American camp alone included the State Department, the Defense Department (representing the U.S. military), the commercial fleet, Congress, labor unions (representing Canal Zone workers), and the American people. And not all of these groups had the same interests.

Bunker's style was decidedly different from the hard-line approach used by previous U.S. negotiators. He chatted easily with the Panamanian negotiators, entertained them at informal lunches, and socialized with them at parties. Instead of presenting hard-and-fast positions, Bunker asked negotiators on each side to find areas where they could agree.

Bunker decided to keep the negotiations secret until a draft treaty had been agreed to by both sides. He knew the American public opposed the idea of "giving away" the canal, and he didn't want a public debate on the issue before negotiators had had a chance to work through their disagreements.

On November 26, 1973, Bunker and Panama's For-

Five percent of the world's commerce passes through the Panama Canal. During the debate over the canal treaties, Americans opposed the idea of "giving away" the waterway.

eign Minister Tack met to discuss Panama's concerns. During a six-day negotiating session beginning on New Year's Day, 1974, the two teams worked out eight areas on which they believed they could agree.

The Tack-Kissinger Statement of Principles, signed February 4, 1974, stipulated that the new treaty negotiations would address the following:

1. The treaty of 1903 would be abandoned.
2. U.S. sovereignty over the Canal Zone would end at some time in the future.
3. Jurisdiction over the Canal Zone territory would pass from the United States to Panama shortly after the new treaty went into effect.
4. The United States would continue to have the

right to use the surrounding land, water, and air to run the canal.

5. Panama would receive a fair share of the tolls from the canal.

6. During the lifetime of the treaty, Panama would gradually increase its participation in operating the canal. At the end of the treaty, Panama would assume total responsibility for the canal.

7. Both the United States and Panama would have the right to defend the canal.

8. Provisions would be made to enlarge the canal if necessary.[7]

The negotiators began by focusing on the areas that were easiest to resolve. For Panama, the most important step was to regain its sovereignty over the Canal Zone territory as soon as possible. Panamanians also wanted to receive more money from the canal, funds that would help jump-start the nation's faltering economy. The United States wanted to ensure that the canal remained neutral—open to all—and that Americans retained the right to defend the canal if it should be threatened.

Tack and Bunker signed papers November 6, 1974, which outlined the initial agreements. Panama would take over responsibility for policing the Canal Zone and would begin operating the courts and criminal justice system within three years after the treaty became valid. A joint board of Panamanian and U.S. delegates would ensure that the canal remained neutral. The two nations would jointly operate and defend the canal in the years the treaty remained in effect. Panamanian workers would be trained to run the canal so they would be prepared to take over the operation once the treaty expired.

WARRING FACTIONS

The State Department supported the initial agreements, but the Department of Defense strongly objected to the idea of a joint defense of the canal. Military leaders warned that the Senate wouldn't support a treaty that did not allow the United States to take action to defend the canal with or without Panama's approval.

When the terms of the agreement leaked out, members of Congress and the public immediately attacked the negotiations, just as Bunker had feared would happen. Southern conservative Senator Strom Thurmond (R-S.C.) announced he had persuaded thirty-seven senators to block the pact if it were presented for ratification. In the House, Representative Marion Gene Snyder (R-Ky.) introduced a bill to prohibit State Department funds from being spent on any negotiations that would sacrifice U.S. rights in the Canal Zone. The legislation didn't pass, but treaty opponents broadcast their message loud and clear.

U.S. President Gerald Ford, who had taken over as president in 1974 when Nixon resigned amid the Watergate scandal, stayed out of the fray. He told the State Department and the Defense Department to work out the matter between them. While many in the Pentagon opposed any move to change the status quo, army officials, who had witnessed the flag riots of 1964 and the growing hostilities against the United States, had long been convinced that a new treaty was needed. It was the only way, they believed, to ease relations with Panama. They argued that the United States did not need to *own* the canal. What was important, they said, was the right to *use* the canal.[8] While the canal remained important for commercial uses, they noted, it was no longer vital to national security. Since the beginning of the Korean War, U.S. Navy aircraft carriers, built to accommodate landing strips for jet fighters, would not fit through the locks of the canal. The Navy had solved the problem by establishing two fleets, one in the Atlantic and one in the Pacific.

Persuaded by these arguments, the Defense Department agreed to participate in the treaty process. An army officer, representing military interests, was appointed to the negotiating team in November 1975.

More Support for Panama

Torrijos got another boost for his country in August 1975 when a conference of nonaligned nations meeting in Peru voted to support Panama's claims to the canal. When negotiations resumed in September, a newly confident Panamanian team brought high expectations to the table. They were surprised when U.S. negotiators asked to retain the right to defend the canal for the next fifty years.

President Ford ordered the talks to be put on hold in 1976. He and other Republican leaders did not want the Panama Canal treaty to dominate the upcoming presidential elections.

Despite the halt in negotiations, the canal played a role in the U.S. presidential campaign. Ronald Reagan, campaigning for the Republican nomination against

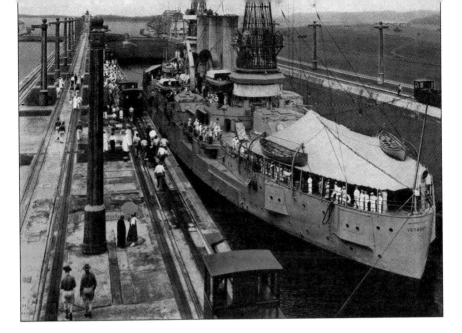

The USS Vermont *goes through the Gatun Locks around 1918. The Panama Canal played a vital role during World War I and World War II by allowing U.S. Navy ships to travel quickly from the Atlantic to the Pacific. But by the 1950s, many Navy ships were too large to fit through the canal.*

Ford, appealed to conservatives by attacking the treaty, accusing Ford of giving away the canal. Ford and Democratic contender Jimmy Carter both supported a new treaty.

Carter, elected by a slim majority, set talks in motion as soon as he took office in January 1977. He retained Bunker as chief negotiator and appointed ambassador Sol M. Linowitz to assist him. Cutting through red tape, Carter gave the negotiators free reign to hammer out a treaty. Throughout the process, Carter met with key senators to brief them on the progress of the talks.

By February, the negotiators had resolved all points except the two toughest: the right of the United States to defend the canal and the assurance that the canal would stay neutral. The U.S. team argued that America had to keep its military bases in the Canal Zone to defend the canal from attack. Panama wanted U.S. soldiers and bases off its soil. Both nations supported the neutrality of the canal, but the United States wanted the right—with or without Panama's permission—to use force if necessary to keep it open.

Pleasing both sides in the negotiations, General Torrijos was quoted as saying, was like trying to meet the demands of the "princess who had big feet and asked a shoemaker to find her a shoe small on the outside and large inside."9

Finally, the two sides reached agreement. The United States would pull its troops out of the Canal Zone when the treaty expired, but it would retain the right to defend the canal forever. Both nations agreed to a separate treaty that would guarantee the neutrality of the canal.

On August 19, 1977, President Carter announced the negotiating team's success. Negotiators worked until September 6 to iron out last-minute details.

HARDER THAN BUILDING THE CANAL

On September 7, 1977, twenty-six heads of state from most of the Latin American nations gathered at the Washington, D.C., headquarters of the Organization of American States as Carter and Panamanian leader General Torrijos signed the two canal treaties. Negotiations had stretched over thirteen years, longer than it had taken the United States to build the canal.

The signing, Carter said, represented "a major step

toward strengthening of relations among the nations of the Western Hemisphere."[10] U.S. leaders representing the four administrations that had worked on the treaty attended the ceremony. Among them were former President Gerald Ford, Lady Bird Johnson (widow of the late Lyndon B. Johnson), former Secretary of State William Rogers (who had served in the Nixon years), Henry Kissinger (secretary of state to both Nixon and Ford), and Carter's secretary of state, Cyrus Vance.

The first pact, the Panama Canal Treaty, ended the 1903 treaty and gave Panama sovereignty over all lands within the Canal Zone. Over the course of the treaty, the United States would gradually transfer responsibilities for running the canal to Panama. When the treaty expired on December 31, 1999, Panama would assume full control over the canal and its operation.

While the treaty was in effect, the United States would continue to use the area around the canal to run and maintain the waterway. A joint agency made up of Americans and Panamanians—the Panama Canal Commission—would administer the canal. Initially, an American chief assisted by a Panamanian deputy would head the commission. In 1990, a Panamanian would assume the top post, with an American deputy. The president of the United States would appoint the commission members.

Panama would eventually be in charge of the police and court system and have jurisdiction over all the former Canal Zone with the exception of the area around the canal administered by the Panama Canal Commission. The host country would get thirty cents per ton of shipping that passed through the canal and would receive a yearly payment of $10 million. It would collect additional fees if the canal made more money than expected. Overall, the treaty would boost Panama's annual take from $2.3 million to an estimated $60 million.[11]

Both nations agreed to examine the need for a new canal together. The treaty gave the United States the right to defend the canal, to increase its armed forces, and to use its military bases in the former Canal Zone until the year 2000. At that time, America would turn over its bases to Panama and withdraw its troops.

The Neutrality Treaty guaranteed that the canal would stay open to ships of all nations. The treaty gave both the United States and Panama the right to "take any action necessary for the maintenance of the neutrality of the Canal."[12] It also stipulated that in a crisis the military ships of both nations would be allowed to pass through the canal without delay.

The signing completed, Carter and Torrijos set out to convince their fellow citizens to support the treaties. Before becoming effective, the treaties had to be approved, or ratified, by both nations. Torrijos had a much easier time of it. In Panama, treaties had to be ratified by a majority of the voters. Some Panamanians protested that their country should receive more money during the life of the treaty. They also believed that the United States should not be allowed to stay until the year 2000. Nevertheless, less than two months after the formal signing, on October 23, the citizens of Panama approved the canal treaties by a two-to-one margin.

Carter, on the other hand, would face his toughest battle yet in the struggle to win ratification.

Chapter Seven

FIGHT FOR RATIFICATION

We bought it, we paid for it, it's ours.[1]
—Ronald Reagan, referring to the Panama Canal

We do not own the Panama Canal Zone. We have never had sovereignty over it. We have only had the right to use it.[2]
—President Jimmy Carter

The effort to ratify the Panama Canal treaties would require every ounce of political strength President Carter possessed. A political outsider who had few ties in Washington, Carter had to enlist the support of leaders of both parties to argue his cause. Determined to push the treaty through, he spent months lobbying individual members of the Senate, making deals, and trading favors to win the crucial votes necessary for ratification.

Under the U.S. Constitution, two-thirds of the Senate—sixty-seven members—are required to ratify a treaty. In the case of the Panama Canal treaties, the U.S. House of Representatives played a role as well. Article Four of the Constitution gives the House and the Senate joint authority to rule on the transfer of U.S. territory or property. The House is also responsible for allocating money, which would be necessary if the treaties were approved.

STATEMENTS ANGER UNITED STATES

Before the two leaders had even signed the treaties, statements made by the Panamanian negotiator had the Senate in an uproar. On August 19, 1977, Dr. Rómulo Escobar Bethancourt had told the Assembly of Corregimiento that the neutrality pact did not give the United States "the right to intervene....What we are giving them is an assurance that the Canal will remain permanently neutral, that we are not going to close the Canal to their ships or those of any other country."[3] Several days later Dr. Bethancourt noted that the treaty did not allow the United States to determine when a violation of neutrality occurred at the canal. He further stated that in an emergency U.S. defense ships would not necessarily be put ahead of other ships going through the canal, but they would be allowed to transit "as quickly as possible."

Senate Majority Leader Howard Baker led the attack during hearings before the Senate's Foreign Relations Committee on September 26. Bethancourt's statements, he said, threatened U.S. interests in the canal. The United States, he argued, should be able to decide when

A sailboat goes through the Miraflores Locks. During treaty negotiations, both Panama and the United States agreed that the Panama Canal should remain open to all.

the canal's neutrality was being violated and should be able to act in such a case. U.S. ships should go ahead of others in an emergency, he added. He couldn't support the treaties, he warned, without such assurances.

With the ratification of the treaties in jeopardy, Carter and Torrijos issued a "Statement of Understanding" on October 14 to address the Senate's concerns. The document gave both countries the right to defend the canal "against any threat to…neutrality."[4] It also gave U.S. and Panamanian defense ships the right to "go to the head of the line" at the canal in an emergency. To ease Panama's fears of an American invasion, the statement stipulated that the United States had no right to intervene in Panama's internal affairs. U.S. military units were to take action only to defend the canal. Such actions would "never be directed against the territorial integrity or political independence of Panama."[5]

ON THE PUBLIC RELATIONS TRAIL

Although the statement did not satisfy the treaties' critics, the Senate continued hearings on the pacts. Six months of political intrigue, arm-twisting, and lengthy debate followed. At the start of the debate, polls showed 80 percent of Americans opposed the treaty. The White House set out to change that with an all-out media and public relations blitz. Without the support of the American public, administration officials knew, the Senate would not vote for ratification.

Dozens of officials served on the White House public relations team, among them press secretary Jody Powell, National Security Council staff member Gerald Schecter, special assistant Frank B. Moore, and congressional liaison Douglas Bennet. Secretary of State Cyrus Vance headed a group of twenty-five officials from the State Department who spoke at more than one hundred events nationwide during the long campaign. Ambassador Bunker did his part, speaking to the public in more than twenty cities in ten states. Negotiator Sol Linowitz urged ratification of the treaties in thirty-five speeches throughout the country.

The bipartisan Committee of Americans for the Canal Treaties, which included Kissinger and former President Ford among its members, joined the push. New Directions, a liberal foreign policy lobbying group, urged supporters to write to their senators in support of the treaties.

They were joined by the National Chamber of Commerce, the American Institute of Merchant Shippers, and the Council of the Americas, which represented the major U.S. firms doing business in Latin America. By January 1978, representatives of the White House had made more than six hundred public appearances on behalf of ratification.

"PANAMA CANAL TRUTH SQUAD"

Those opposed to the treaties conducted their own cross-country media campaign. The Committee for the Survival of a Free Congress, a group that supported conservative causes, sponsored speakers against the treaties. Joining in the opposition effort were several other conservative groups, the Conservative Caucus, the American Conservative Union, Citizens for the Republic, the Young Republicans, and the Council for National Defense. In January, opponents to the treaties organized a five-day blitz of the nation to push their views. Dubbed the "Panama Canal Truth Squad," the group, which included members of the House and Senate as well as retired military officers, spoke in seven cities and covered almost 7,000 miles (11,300 km). A member of the squad, former California Governor Ronald Reagan, spoke before a Denver crowd as part of the tour.

During initial negotiations, the Defense Department had sided with the antitreaty forces. But eventually Defense officials dropped their opposition, and the Joint Chiefs of Staff endorsed the treaties. While Secretary of Defense Harold Brown joined other administration officials on the speech-making circuit, individual officers, most of whom had retired, spoke out against the treaties. Three prominent military men—Admiral Thomas H. Moorer, former chair of the Joint Chiefs of Staff; Admiral John S. McCain Jr., former Navy commander of the Pacific fleet; and Lieutenant General Daniel O. Graham, former director of the Defense Intelligence Agency—joined the Truth Squad tour to oppose ratification. They argued that a shift in power at the canal would jeopardize U.S. security and help the Soviets get a firmer foothold in Latin America.

LEADERSHIP ON BOARD

Early in January, Minority Leader Baker met with General Torrijos during a tour of the canal. Baker said he would support the treaties only if amendments spelled out the guarantees outlined in the Statement of Understanding signed in October. After Torrijos reluctantly agreed to the amendments, Baker announced his support of ratification. It was a crucial vote for the pro-treaty forces. By mid-January, Majority Leader Robert Byrd announced his support, with the same reservations expressed by Baker. With the two Senate leaders on board, the ratification bill had bipartisan support. On January 30, the Foreign Relations Committee voted 14 to 1 in favor of ratification and sent the treaties to the full Senate for debate.

President Carter kicked off the Senate debate with an address of his own to the American people. Seated before a fire in the White House library, Carter outlined the ben-

A view of Miraflores Locks on the Pacific side of the canal. President Carter said turning the canal over to Panama was the right and fair thing to do.

efits of the treaties point by point. He said ratification was in the "highest national interest of the United States."[6] The 22-minute speech rebutted all arguments against the treaties and concluded by saying that Theodore Roosevelt would endorse the decision of "a great and generous people with a national strength and wisdom to do what is right for us and what is fair to others."[7]

For the next ten weeks—the longest debate on a foreign policy issue since the Versailles Treaty hearings in 1919–1920—Senators argued the pros and cons of the treaties. Senators opposed to ratification proposed seventy-nine amendments, most designed to anger Panama and ensure the ultimate defeat of the treaties. Senator James B. Allen (D-Ala.), one of the leading opponents, proposed an amendment that would have allowed the

United States to keep troops in Panama after 2000 if the American president decided it was necessary. The Panamanians had vehemently opposed such a proposal during treaty negotiations. The amendment was defeated.

GAVEL-TO-GAVEL COVERAGE

National Public Radio broadcast the entire debate beginning with the first rap of the gavel on February 8. It was the first time in history the Senate had allowed radio coverage of its proceedings. As the radio audience listened, senators provided a constant barrage of arguments, not always without humor. In one exchange, Senator Daniel Moynihan (D-N.Y.) attempted to describe colonialism to Senator Carl Curtis (R-Neb.). Explaining that the treaties would dispel America's past colonialism toward Panama, Moynihan suggested that Curtis remove his boots, jacket, and necktie and give up his desk if he wanted to know what it felt like to live under colonial rule. "The fine desk that Calhoun himself may have used, would the Senator take that away?" Moynihan asked Curtis. "We have some orange crates for the Senator."[9]

Opinions on the treaties varied widely. Proponents like Assistant Majority Leader Alan Cranston (D-Calif.) said the best way to keep the canal open was to ratify the treaties. Such an action, he said, would "demonstrate to the world that we have the real, inner strength of the truly powerful, not the false bravado of the fearful bully."[10] Senator Frank Church (D-Idaho), agreed, saying the treaties would help prevent the spread of communism in Latin America.

Senator Paul Laxalt (R-Nev.), one of the opposition leaders, argued the opposite, saying the Cubans or the Soviets would try to take over the area if the U.S. loosened its control of the canal. Senator John C. Stennis (D-Miss.) quoted a study he said showed that the treaties would cost U.S. taxpayers $2 billion in lost revenue.

The radio broadcasts coupled with the Herculean push by both sides to make their views known captured the attention of the public. According to *New York Times* columnist Tom Wicker, senators were receiving 150,000 cards and letters a day during the canal debate, far more than the usual amount.[11] A January 1978 poll showed public approval of the treaties had risen to 45 percent, with 42 percent still opposed.[12]

On March 12, the Senate approved the amendments incorporating the Statement of Understanding (called the Leadership Amendments) that Baker and Byrd had demanded in exchange for their support. As the Senate headed for a final vote on the Neutrality Treaty, the tally was 62 in favor, five short of the needed two-thirds. In a last-minute push, Carter met with wavering senators and promised them support for favored legislation in return for a yes vote on the treaty. His efforts changed the minds of three or four more senators, still not enough to pass the ratification bill.[13]

RESERVATIONS

Two powerful Democrats—Senator Dennis DeConcini of Arizona and Senator Sam Nunn of Georgia—continued to hold out. DeConcini wanted the Senate to add an amendment that gave the United States the right to use military force to reopen the canal even if the closing was due to a strike or other domestic problem. Nunn wanted both countries to have the option to agree to station U.S. troops in Panama after 2000 if "circumstances required it."[14] Proponents had no choice but to accept the two amendments, even though they feared Panama would reject the new wording.

Carter had given the effort all he had, and it paid off. On April 18, 1978, the Senate voted 68 to 32 to ratify the Neutrality Treaty with the two amendments attached. After all their hard work to win support, the treaty proponents had one vote to spare.

As expected, Torrijos objected to the amendments and threatened to reject the entire package. He believed the DeConcini Amendment overrode the assurances in the Leadership Amendments that protected Panama from U.S. meddling. The White House set to work to forge a compromise between the Senate and the Panamanian leader. On April 16 both sides agreed to add a clarifying statement that reiterated the assurances against U.S. intervention. The statement noted that a U.S. action to open the canal "shall not have as its purpose nor be interpreted as a right of intervention." It further stated that the treaty gave the United States no right to interfere with Panama's "political independence or sovereign integrity."[15]

With the Senate about to vote on the Panama Canal Treaty, Majority Leader Byrd knelt in front of a coffee table in Senator Church's office in the Capitol and dashed off the final words of the compromise.[16] Senators passed the statement by a vote of 73 to 27. The roll call for the treaty began at 6 P.M. Senator Byrd passed when his name was first called so that he could cast the 67th—and deciding—vote. In the end, the senators, once again, voted 68 to 32 to ratify the treaty.

A "NEW ERA"

Carter hailed the vote as the "beginning of a new era" in U.S. foreign relations.[17] By ratifying the treaties, he said, the United States sent a signal to the world that it would deal with small nations "on the basis of mutual respect and partnership."[18]

Treaty critics issued harshly worded warnings after the vote. Senator Robert Griffin (R-Mich.) called the treaty "a dangerous step, a gamble for the United States and the security of the United States."[19] Ronald Reagan said he was disappointed by the vote and believed it was "a very extreme case of ignoring the sentiment of the people of our country."[20]

In Panama, Torrijos proclaimed the ratification as "one of the greatest and most awaited triumphs" in the nation's history.[21] Crowds gathered in the streets as fireworks exploded in celebration. Many Panamanians, however, had begun to question the treaties after the last-minute amendments, the long delay in ratifying the treaty, and the worsening economy. Torrijos, looking to whip up enthusiasm for the treaties among his people, proclaimed April 20 a national holiday. The general told reporters that if the Senate had not ratified the treaties, "Panama would have begun the struggle for liberation

General Omar Torrijos of Panama hugs U.S. President Jimmy Carter after signing the Panama Canal treaties in Panama City on July 16, 1978.

and possibly by tomorrow the canal would no longer be functioning."[22]

The action represented a major shift in American power, particularly in Latin America. As a potent demonstration of U.S. goodwill, the treaties improved relations with Panama and other Latin American nations.

In the United States, the treaties and the battle to ratify them had political consequences that would be felt for years. Though Carter rejoiced over the ratification, the small margin of victory and the effort expended left him with little leverage for future battles. He had tapped all his resources dry in the effort to ratify the Panama Canal treaties, and he would pay the price later. When it came time to seek support for an upcoming arms control treaty, the Strategic Arms Limitations Talks (SALT) pact, Carter found he had little left to promise wavering senators. The SALT treaty went down in defeat.[23]

The treaty battle affected the political careers of others as well. Senator Baker, who had led the pro-treaty forces along with Senator Byrd, lost the backing of conservatives in his bid to be the Republican nominee for president in 1980. Ronald Reagan, an outspoken critic of the treaties, won the GOP nomination and the presidency with the help of conservative supporters.

Carter traveled to Panama City for the official signing of the ratified treaties on June 16, 1978. After putting their signatures on the documents, Carter and Torrijos rose and shook hands as the watching dignitaries applauded. Overcome by joy, Torrijos reached over and gave a surprised Carter a hug.

Chapter Eight

INVASION

We're grateful to the U.S. for throwing Noriega out. But no one wants a stranger running his house. Let's hope Panamanians can control their own country again soon.[1]
   —Panamanian student on "Operation Just Cause"

On October 1, 1979, General Wallace Nutting, commander of the U.S. Southern Command, made his way to ceremonies marking the transfer of the Canal Zone to Panama. Thousands of people lined the route along the way. "I've never seen so many people," Nutting recalls. "Every face was smiling. It was marvelous."[2]

Nutting, who had arrived in Panama the previous Friday, prepared to sign the documents that would turn the Canal Zone over to Panama. Vice-President Walter Mondale, on hand for the ceremonies, joked to the audience,

From left, Panama President Arístedes Royo, an unidentified soldier, Colonel Florencio Florez (commander of Panama's National Guard), U.S. Vice-President Walter Mondale, and U.S. General Wallace Nutting at the implementation of the Panama Canal treaties October 1, 1979, in Panama.

"General Nutting has been here only three days and already he's given away the canal."[3]

Many people believed the United States made a mistake in agreeing to the treaties. Before General Nutting left for Panama, a German officer grabbed his sleeve and advised, only half jokingly, "Don't give away the Panama Canal." General Nutting himself views the transfer of the canal to Panama as "one of the most magnanimous acts in history," especially because Americans have treasured the canal as a symbol of U.S. achievement for decades.[4]

Improved Relations

During Nutting's tour of duty in Panama, he witnessed the impact of the treaty and became convinced that the transfer benefited the United States and helped promote democracy. "It relieved a tremendous amount of political pressure between the United States and the countries of Latin America," Nutting says. The passage of the treaties, he says, kept Panama "out of the communists' grasp" at a time when Communist insurgents were leading rebellions in other Central American nations.[5]

"[The treaties] gave the United States credibility," says Nutting. "People began to see the U.S. as someone they could trust."[6]

An incident on January 9, 1980, served to demonstrate the improving relations between Americans and Panama. On that day, Panamanians planned to march past Balboa High School to celebrate Martyrs' Day in memory of those who had died during the flag riots of 1964. U.S. officials feared the march might erupt in violence, but a parade permit was granted. "There was no legal reason to keep them out," Nutting said. The paraders marched to the school, held a ceremony at the flagpole, and returned peacefully to their homes.[7]

Tough Times

Though relations with the United States remained calm, Panama was seething with domestic strife. The passage of the canal treaties had not brought Panama the boost to its economy that had been expected. In 1980, one-fifth of Panama's workers couldn't find jobs. Inflation rose, farms produced a poor harvest, and strikes shut down 80 percent of the nation's industries for two days. Panama, with just 2 million people, owed $5.5 billion to foreign nations. In relation to its population, it was the largest national debt in the world.[8]

The year 1980 began well politically. In the first free elections since Torrijos took control in 1968, the voters elected a National Assembly. Although Torrijos' party, the PRD, retained control, representatives from several political parties won seats on the assembly. Torrijos' protégé, Arístedes Royo, named president in 1978, won re-election.

The following year, Torrijos was killed in a plane crash, and in 1982 the National Guard forced Royo to resign. General Manuel Noriega, who had served as Torrijos' intelligence officer, began to exert his power as head of the National Guard. Royo's successor and four subsequent presidents served at Noriega's will.

Noriega used information he had obtained as head of intelligence to blackmail Panama's leaders and gain control.[9] Corrupt and money-hungry, Noriega worked for both the guerrillas and the government forces in Nicaragua, was on the payroll of the U.S. Central Intelligence Agency, worked with the Soviets and the Cubans, had ties to Israel spies, and connections with the U.S. Drug Enforcement Administration.[10] It was his role as a drug smuggler for Colombia's drug lords, however, that finally brought him down. "A bad hombre,"[11] in Nutting's words.

In early 1988, a Miami court indicted Noriega on

General Manuel Noriega celebrates the defeat of an attempted coup to remove him from power.

drug charges. When Noriega refused to step down from power, the United States issued sanctions against Panama. All U.S. payments to the country were stopped. The actions triggered a crisis in Panama, where one-fifth of the work force was on the U.S. payroll. Out-of-work Panamanians staged protests, and Noriega put the country on a state of national alert.

When voters elected Guillermo Endara as president in a May 7, 1989, election by a three-to-one margin, Noriega nullified the election. Pro-Noriega thugs beat the president and his two vice-presidents, sending Endara to the hospital.

As the crisis continued, relations between the United States and Panama worsened. In October 1989, a coup led by disgruntled Panamanian military officers failed to depose Noriega. U.S. President George Bush ordered all ships registered under Panama's flag banned from American ports.

On Friday, December 15, 1989, the National Assembly, under Noriega's control, declared Panama in a state of war with the United States, accusing Americans of meddling in Panamanian affairs. The following day, an unarmed U.S. Army officer was shot and killed while walking in Panama City. The incident was the last straw for American leaders concerned over escalating violence in Panama and eager to remove Noriega from power.

MARINES LAND

Beginning at 1 A.M. December 20, 1989, twenty-four thousand U.S. paratroopers, infantry, and marines stormed downtown Panama City. Backed by helicopter gunships, the soldiers bombarded the El Chorrillo section of the city, where Noriega's headquarters were based. Tanks rolled down city streets, and soldiers parachuted to the ground amid artillery fire. The U.S. forces dropped 422 bombs on the city and seized power stations and the international airport.

During the bombing, the United States closed the canal for the first time in history. It was reopened after

Cathedral Church and Plaza, Panama City. The city was the site of an invasion by U.S. troops in 1989 aimed at removing Manuel Noriega from power.

the main fighting had ceased. In the next day and a half, American soldiers occupied the isthmus and crushed Panamanian forces still loyal to Noriega. President Bush declared the invasion a success. The crafty Noriega, however, escaped.

Shortly before the invasion, a Panamanian judge swore into office Endara and his vice-presidents, Ricardo Arias Calderón and Guillermo Ford, at a U.S. military base near the canal. They remained in hiding while Noriega was on the run.

The United States offered a $1 million reward for Noriega's capture. He eventually sought refuge in the home of the Roman Catholic Church's top official in Panama. For the next few days, U.S. forces blasted the residence with heavy metal rock music broadcast over powerful speakers. The church told Noriega he would have to leave, and the general surrendered to U.S. officers. Convicted of drug smuggling in a Miami court, he is now serving a forty-year prison sentence in the United States.

PANAMANIANS CHEER

Latin American nations condemned the invasion. But most Panamanians supported the U.S. action. They stood on street corners and cheered as U.S. troops marched into their country. Polls later showed more than three-quarters of Panama's citizens favored the U.S. actions.

"My reaction was 'Thank God, at last,'" said Luis Martinz, a Panamanian who opposed Noriega, the day after the bombing attack. "I don't know how patriotic that sounds, but the situation had gotten very nasty recently."[12]

Responding to critics, Bush said he ordered the attack to restore democracy in Panama and to protect American lives there. He cited the Panama Canal agreement signed by Carter and Torrijos in 1977 giving both countries the right to defend the canal "against any threat to the regime of neutrality" and granting them "the right to act against any aggression or threat directed against the canal."

Opponents noted that the agreement also stated the

Panamanian aid workers help residents of the El Chorrillo section of Panama City find housing after the U.S. invasion of Panama destroyed their homes. The mural in the background depicts the damage from the attack and tells people that they should "never forget."

United States had no right to intervene "in the internal affairs of Panama" and that no action should be "directed against the territorial integrity or political independence of Panama." The General Assembly of the United Nations condemned the invasion by a vote of 75 to 20. The Organization of American States did the same, voting 20 to 1 against the action.[13]

The U.S. Congress supported Bush, but a few leaders spoke out against the Panama incursion. Representative Don Edwards (D-Calif.) said the U.S. action "appears to be a trigger-happy act of gunboat diplomacy that continues our mindless one-hundred-year abuse of small Central American nations."[14]

The invasion, dubbed "Operation Just Cause" by the U.S. government, left Panama in shambles. Three hundred to five hundred Panamanians died in the attack, and thousands more were injured. Estimates of damage caused by the action ranged up to $2 billion. Looters, raiding the shops in Panama City, caused an additional $500 million in losses.[15] When the attack ended, twenty thousand people had no homes, and a third of Panama's people were without jobs.[16]

Chapter Nine

COUNTDOWN TO **1999**

At this moment, nothing is more important than the
administration of the Panama Canal.[1]
   —Joaquin Vallarino, Panamanian businessman

G uillermo Endara faced great obstacles when
he assumed power as president of Panama on
December 20, 1989. He didn't even have a
desk or office supplies in the looted government buildings of Panama City. Aid from the United States was
delayed for six months. Thousands remained homeless.
Almost 90 percent of the shopkeepers in Panama's capital city had been besieged by looters. Many had not
reopened their shops.

In the year following the invasion, the United States
paid $452 million in economic aid to Panama. With an
additional $500 million in loans and guarantees, the aid

package was the third largest given by Americans to any nation in the world.[2] The money was used for food and for housing, to create jobs, train police, and aid looted businesses.

While most Panamanians supported the U.S. ouster of Noriega, the aftermath left them frustrated and angry. A year after the attack, almost five thousand people were still living in tentlike cubicles inside a U.S. aircraft hangar in Balboa. Most had lost their homes when U.S. bombs were dropped on the slums of Panama City. Church worker Robert Melville described the scene inside the hangar:

> Typically a family of five or six live in a partitioned space the size of our dining room. Breakfast is three pieces of white bread, a dab of margarine, and a cup of weak coffee or tea. There is milk for children under 6 only. There is no lunch.[3]

Some Panamanians believed the invasion had been planned as a way for the United States to alter the Panama Canal treaties. They believed Americans would use the incident as an excuse to keep U.S. troops in Panama indefinitely. As time went on, however, it seemed that Americans intended to keep their word when it came to the treaties.

NEW LEADER

Endara proved to be an ineffective leader, described by opponents as "a non-musician leading an orchestra that does not play."[4] Panamanians split their vote three

Colón, above, has some of the worst slums in Latin America.

ways in the 1994 election. As a result Ernesto Pérez Balladares, a member of Noriega's PRD party, won the presidency with only a third of the vote.

Under Balladares' leadership, Panama has made progress in reforming its economy and strengthening its government. In 1994, Panamanians abolished the army that had propped up dictators and despots for so many years. The United States has helped train the civilian police force, though many Panamanians still fear former Noriega cronies they say are members of the force.

Problems remain. Panama continues to be plagued by poverty, especially in city slums and in rural areas. There is "an incredible contrast" between the cosmopolitan banking centers in Panama City and the subsistence living of the farmers in the interior of Panama,[5] according to Episcopal Church worker Barbara Melville. While in Panama, she helped establish a program similar to the U.S. Head Start program for Panamanian youngsters.

Literacy among Panamanians as a whole is about 88 percent, but Melville estimates a quarter of rural residents can't read or write, and another quarter can read only at elementary level, sometimes only their names. "There are no books, no papers, no TVs," she says of the rural areas. "Some of the kids in the school used crayons and pencils for the first time."[6]

Melville met people in the interior villages who had never seen the Panama Canal, even though it was only about 20 miles (32 km) away. For them, she said, "the Panama Canal might as well be in Africa."[7]

DON'T SINK THE SHIP

Corruption and political instability continue to be worries. President Balladares raised eyebrows when he sought to change the constitution to allow himself to seek another term in 1999. By law, Panama's presidents can serve only one five-year term. Balladares said he was "not animated by any personal ambition other than that of completing a task undertaken that is already beginning to show results."[8] But opponents feared Balladares wanted to cash in when Panama takes over the canal.

Panamanian citizens turned down Balladares' request for a constitutional amendment in a two-to-one vote August 30, 1998. They will vote for a new president May 2, 1999.

Balladares had talked with the United States about setting up a multinational antidrug center in Panama. The plan would have allowed two thousand U.S. troops to remain in Panama after the treaty expires. With the vote against Balladares, it was doubtful the center would be opened. The center had been proposed, in part, to help ease the loss of almost $400 million the U.S. spends in Panama each year. But many Panamanians objected to a longer stay by the U.S. military. "How to let go of [U.S. involvement] without sinking their own economic ship is the problem,"[9] notes church worker Robert Melville.

As the time draws closer to December 31, 1999, observers watch and wait to see how Panama will manage the canal. "I see no reason why Panama shouldn't be able

Church worker Barbara Melville, left, instructs children in a rural Panamanian village.

to run it as efficiently as we have—as long as it's not politi-cized,"[10] says General Nutting.

The new administration, to be elected just four months before the treaty expires, will supervise the canal transfer and decide what to do with the land and build-ings gained in the deal. The property is worth more than $3.5 billion and includes 5,500 buildings and 93,000 acres (37,600 ha) of land.

Panama has set up the Interoceanic Regional Author-ity to develop the properties after the transfer. The group has outlined plans to open hotels, develop the port, set up tourist attractions, and establish more export zones. An estimated $800 million has been allocated for the development.

MOST PROMISING FUTURE?

Among the projects is a tourist center atop Ancon Hill. The Interoceanic Regional Authority has requested proposals from companies interested in bidding on the project. Officials envision an aerial tram that will carry vis-itors to the summit, where they can dine in a hilltop restaurant, stop at the gift shop, and sit awhile in the botanical garden and bird sanctuary. Below, the world's great ships will be steaming through an efficient, impres-sive Panama Canal—still an amazing engineering feat and a witness to Panama's most promising future. That is Panama's vision and the hope of all those involved in world trade.

Source Notes

Introduction: Home at Last

1. Interview with General Wallace Nutting, Sept. 9, 1998.

Chapter One: Contract for Controversy

1. Woodard, Colin, "Panama: Life after the Zone," *The Bulletin of the Atomic Scientists*, September/October 1997, 14.
2. Woodard, 13.
3. "Panama Two Years after Operation Just Cause," *U.S. Department of State Dispatch*, Feb. 10, 1992, vol. 3, no. 6, 96.
4. Woodard, 14.
5. Dostert, Pierre Etienne, *Latin America: 1997, The World Today Series*, 31st ed. (Harpers Ferry, West Virginia: Stryker-Post Publications, 1997), 179.
6. Serrill, Michael S., "The Canal Cronies," *Time*, Dec. 15, 1997, vol. 150, no. 25, 56–57.
7. Posey, Carl, "The Bittersweet Memory that was the Canal Zone," *Smithsonian*, November 1991, vol. 22, no. 8, 175.
8. Serrill, "The Canal Cronies," 56.
9. Dostert, 178.
10. Serrill, Michael S., "Panama: The Big Switch," *Time*, Dec. 15, 1997, vol. 150, no. 25, 56.
11. Woodard, 13.
12. Posey, 178.
13. Ibid.

14. Interview with Robert Melville, Aug. 19, 1998.

15. Nutting interview.

16. Woodard, 13.

17. Serrill, Michael S., "The Canal Cronies," 56.

18. Nutting interview.

CHAPTER TWO: BUILDING A CANAL

1. McCullough, David, *The Path Between the Seas: The Creation of the Panama Canal, 1870–1914* (New York: Simon & Schuster, 1977), 126.

2. Panama Canal Commission, http://www.pananet.com/pancanal/pcc.htm.

3. McCullough, 35.

4. Ibid., 39.

5. Ibid., 37.

6. Ibid., 104.

7. Conniff, Michael L., *Black Labor on a White Canal: Panama, 1904–1981* (Pittsburgh, Pa.: University of Pittsburgh Press, 1985), 3.

8. McCullough, 158.

9. Duval, Miles P. Jr., *And the Mountains Will Move: The Story of the Building of the Panama Canal* (New York: Greenwood Press, 1968), 127.

10. McCullough, 424.

CHAPTER THREE: AMERICANS TAKE OVER

1. Duval, *And the Mountains Will Move*, 228.

2. Treaty of 1846, Article 35, in *Cadiz to Cathay: The Story of the Long Diplomatic Struggle for the Panama Canal* by Miles P. Duval Jr. (New York: Greenwood Press, 1968), 452.

3. *New York Times*, Sept. 13, 1925, 10 XX.

4. The Spooner Act, Sec. 4 in *Cadiz to Cathay*, 498–499.

5. Duval, *Cadiz to Cathay*, 170.

6. Ibid., 262.

7. Ibid., 322.

8. Ibid., 335.

9. *New York Times*, Nov. 4, 1903, 1.

10. Art. II, *Cadiz to Cathay*, 478.

11. Art. III, *Cadiz to Cathay*, 479.

12. *New York Times*, Dec. 3, 1903, 3.

13. McCullough, 400.

14. Ibid., 467.

15. Ibid., 581.

16. Ibid., 582.

17. "How the Big Ditch Was Dug," *Time*, Aug. 22, 1977, 10.

18. Panama Canal Commission.

19. "How the Big Ditch Was Dug," 10.

20. *Cadiz to Cathay*, 438.

CHAPTER FOUR: SIMMERING CONFLICTS

1. Posey, 164–165.

2. *New York Times*, Aug. 16, 1914, Section II, 14.

3. Ibid.

4. *New York Times*, July 16, 1914, 8.

5. *New York Times*, Aug. 16, 1914, Section II, 14.

6. Westerman, George W., *The West Indian Worker on the Canal Zone* (National Civic League, 1951), 12.

7. Ibid.

8. Conniff, 50.

9. Westerman, 25.

10. Conniff, 90.

11. Westerman, 12.

12. Ibid., 14.

13. Conniff, 123.

CHAPTER FIVE: RALLYING AROUND THE FLAG

1. "Panama: Campaigning on the Canal," *Time*, Feb. 7, 1964, 41.

2. *Compton's Encyclopedia*, vol. 22, 292.

3. Conniff, 141.

4. *New York Times*, Jan. 10, 1964, 10.

5. Ibid.

6. Ibid., 1.

7. Conniff, 148.

CHAPTER SIX: NEGOTIATING A NEW TREATY

1. "President Carter's Televised Speech on the Panama Canal Treaties," *New York Times*, Feb. 2, 1978, A14.

2. "Ceding the Canal—Slowly," *Time*, August 22, 1977, 9.

3. Interview with Barbara Melville, Aug. 19, 1998.

4. McDonough, Mark G., "Panama Canal Treaty Negotiations (A): The Setting" (Cambridge, Mass.: Harvard University, 1979), 3. Much of the discussion of the treaty negotiations and ratification relied heavily on McDonough's two papers.

5. Conniff, 151.

6. Stephen B. Young, *LBJ's Strategy for Disengagement*.

7. McDonough, "Panama Canal Treaty Negotiations (A): The Setting," 7–8.

8. Nutting interview.

9. "Ceding the Canal—Slowly," 8.

10. *New York Times*, Sept. 8, 1977, 1A.

11. Dostert, 175.

12. McDonough, Mark G., "Panama Canal Treaty Negotiations (B): Concluding a Treaty" (Cambridge, Mass.: Harvard University, 1979), 6.

CHAPTER SEVEN: FIGHT FOR RATIFICATION

1. *New York Times*, Feb. 2, 1978, A14.

2. Ibid.

3. McDonough, Mark G., "Panama Canal Treaty Negotiations (B): Concluding a Treaty," 6.

4. Ibid., 7.

5. Ibid.

6. *New York Times*, Feb. 2, 1978, A1.

7. *New York Times*, Feb. 2, 1978, A14.

8. Krepon, Michael, and Dan Caldwell, eds., *The Politics of Arms Control Treaty Ratification* (New York: St. Martin's Press, 1991), 296.

9. *New York Times*, March 2, 1978, A10.

10. *New York Times*, Feb. 9, 1978, A1.

11. *New York Times*, Feb. 21, 1978, A31.

12. McDonough, Mark G., "Panama Canal Treaty Negotiations (B): Concluding a Treaty," 11.

13. Ibid., 13.

14. Ibid.

15. Ibid., 15.

16. Ibid. (from the *Washington Post*, April 20, 1978, A3).

17. *New York Times*, April 19, 1978, A1.

18. Ibid.

19. Ibid., A16.

20. Ibid.

21. Ibid., A1.

22. Ibid., A16.

23. Platt, Alan, "The Anti-Ballistic Missile Treaty," in *The Politics of Arms Control Treaty Ratification*, 296.

CHAPTER EIGHT: INVASION

1. Manning, Stephen, "The U.S. Invasion of Panama," *Scholastic Update*, Feb. 9, 1990, vol. 122, no. 11, 8.

2. Nutting interview.

3. Ibid.

4. Ibid.

5. Ibid.

6. Ibid.

7. Ibid.

8. Dostert.

9. Nutting interview.

10. Dostert, 177.

11. Nutting interview.

12. *New York Times*, Dec. 21, 1989, A18.

13. Drinan, Robert F. "Panama invasion is still a shame and a crime," *National Catholic Reporter*, Dec. 18, 1992, vol. 29, no. 8, 12.

14. Bierman, John, "The Panama War," *Maclean's*, Jan. 1, 1990, vol. 103, no. 1, 52.

15. Drinan.

16. Cockburn, Alexander, "Truth and Casualties: Yesterday Panama," *Nation*, Feb 4, 1991, vol. 252, no. 4, 115.

CHAPTER NINE: COUNTDOWN TO 1999

1. Rohter, Larry, "Vote Sunday in Panama Could Affect

Canal's Future," *New York Times*, August 30, 1998 (via Internet).

2. "Panama after Operation Just Cause," Department of State Dispatch, Feb. 4, 1991, vol. 2, no. 5, 78.

3. Melville, Barbara, and Robert Melville, "Letter from Panama," *The Northeast*, Episcopal Diocese of Maine, April–May 1990, 2.

4. Dostert, 178.

5. Barbara Melville interview.

6. Ibid.

7. Ibid.

8. Rohter.

9. Robert Melville interview.

10. Nutting Interview.

GLOSSARY

ALLIANCE FOR PROGRESS. Ten-year economic development program introduced by President John F. Kennedy in 1961 designed to help South American and Central American countries.

ANNEXATION. The act of adding a region to an existing nation.

COMMISSARY. A store operated by the U.S. Army where military personnel and civilian workers hired by the army could buy food and supplies at reduced rates.

CONQUISTADORS. Explorers from Spain or Portugal who conquered the tribes living in Mexico, South America, and Central America during the 1500s and 1600s.

CONTINENTAL DIVIDE. A mountain ridge going acoss a continent; the rivers on one side flow down that side of the ridge, while the rivers on the other side flow down the opposite side of the ridge.

COUP. The taking over of power by a group of people, usually with ties to the military.

DICTATOR. A ruler with absolute power.

EMINENT DOMAIN. The right of the state to seize property or land with or without the consent of the owner; usually the owner is paid for his property.

FREE-TRADE ZONE. An area set aside where businesses can import, store, and export goods without having to pay a tariff or customs fee.

GOLD WORKERS. Those who held administrative positions or performed skilled labor in the Canal Zone; almost exclusively white workers.

GOOD NEIGHBOR POLICY. Plan promoted by President

Franklin D. Roosevelt in the 1930s in which the United States pledged to respect the rights of Latin America and vowed not to interfere in domestic affairs.

GROSS NATIONAL PRODUCT (GNP). The total value of all the goods and services produced by a nation, usually over the course of a year.

GUERRILLAS. Small bands of revolutionaries who attack the government in power.

GUNBOAT DIPLOMACY. Controlling other countries by threatening to wield force; President Theodore Roosevelt and later presidents were accused of gunboat diplomacy in their dealings with Latin America.

INFLATION. Sharp rise in prices of goods.

IN PERPETUITY. Forever. The 1903 Panama Canal treaty gave the United States control over the canal "in perpetuity."

ISTHMUS. A narrow strip of land connecting two larger territories; Panama is an isthmus connecting North and South America.

JURISDICTION. The authority to control an area.

LOCAL RATE. Lower wages paid to non-U.S. citizens working in the Canal Zone, mostly black workers of West Indian descent.

LOCKS. Sections of a canal blocked off with gates. When the gates are opened, water enters and raises ships to the next level. When the water is drained, ships are lowered to the next level.

MALARIA. An often fatal disease carried by mosquitoes that causes chills, fever, and sweating in victims.

MONEY LAUNDERING. Transferring money through various bank accounts so it can't be traced to illegal activities.

NEUTRALITY. Taking no side in a dispute.

PANAMA CANAL AUTHORITY. The group of Panamanians

who will oversee the operation of the Panama Canal as of December 31, 1999.

PANAMA CANAL COMMISSION. The group of Americans and Panamanians overseeing the Panama Canal from 1979 to 1999.

PANAMA CANAL COMPANY. The organization, set up by the U.S. government, in charge of the Panama Canal between 1914 and 1979.

PANAMA CANAL ZONE. The strip of land surrounding the Panama Canal and running through Panama, measuring 10 feet (16 km) wide by 50 miles (80 km) long. The zone, controlled by the United States, was disbanded and the area turned over to Panama in 1979.

PROTECTORATE. A region or country that is under the control and is protected by a larger, more powerful nation.

RATIFY. To approve formally and make valid. The U.S. Senate requires a two-thirds vote to ratify treaties.

RESERVATION. A condition added to an agreement or treaty.

SEA LEVEL CANAL. A trench linking one body of water to another.

SILVER WORKERS. Those who worked as unskilled laborers in the Canal Zone; mostly black West Indian workers.

SLASH-AND-BURN AGRICULTURE. A method of farming in which vegetation is cut down and burned.

SOVEREIGNTY. An independent nation's absolute authority over its territory and its people.

U.S. RATE. Higher wages paid to U.S. citizens working in the Canal Zone, mostly in supervisory or skilled positions.

YELLOW FEVER. An often fatal disease spread by mosquitoes that causes a person to bleed internally and turns the skin and eyes yellow.

FOR FURTHER INFORMATION

BOOKS FOR YOUNG READERS

Culebra Cut (Adventures in Time) by Judith Head, Carolrhoda Books, 1995. The story of a boy and his adventures in Panama in 1911 during the construction of the Panama Canal.

Locks, Crocs, & Skeeters: The Story of the Panama Canal by Nancy W. Parker, Greenwillow Books, 1996. Interesting and well-illustrated book on history, characters, and political leaders involved in the Panama Canal story.

Panama (Enchantment Series) by Ana Maria B. Vazquez, Childrens Press, 1991. A comprehensive look at Panama, its geography, history, economy, and culture.

Panama and the United States: Divided by the Canal by Edmund Lindop, Twenty-first Century Books, 1997. Thorough discussion of the events leading up to the canal's transfer and the current political situation in Panama.

The Panama Canal (Building History Series) by Tim McNeese, Lucent Books, 1997. Personal accounts and pertinent facts tell the story of the Panama Canal.

The Panama Canal: The Story of How a Jungle Was Conquered and the World Made Smaller (Wonders of the World) by Elizabeth Mann, Mikaya Press, 1998. Tales of heroism and hard work by the builders of the Panama Canal.

Panama in Pictures (Visual Geography Series) by Peter English, ed., Lerner Publications, 1987. Illustrations and information on Panama's geography, history, government, people, economy, and culture.

Panama's Canal by Carl R. Oliver, Franklin Watts, 1990. Background and discussion of canal transfer highlighted by personal accounts.

ADULT BOOKS

America's Prisoner: The Memoirs of Manuel Noriega by Manuel Noriega and Peter Eisner, Random House, 1997. Controversial account of Panama under Noriega's rule, his dealings with the CIA, and the U.S. invasion of Panama. Written from his Miami prison cell.

And the Mountains Will Move: The Story of the Building of the Panama Canal by Miles P. Duval Jr., Greenwood Press, 1968. An in-depth history of the Panama Canal, based on original documents and archival material.

Panama's Canal: What Happens When the United States Gives a Small Country What It Wants? by Mark Falcoff, AEI Press, 1998. Political analysis of the transfer of the canal to Panama, its origins, and insights into the future.

The Path Between the Seas: The Creation of the Panama Canal, 1870–1914 by David McCullough, Simon & Schuster, 1977. The dramatic saga of the building of the Panama Canal, written by a first-class historian. Features well-developed characters and fascinating details behind the planning and construction of the canal. The premier history of the Panama Canal.

Portrait of the Panama Canal by William Friar, Graphic Arts Center Pub. Co., 1996. The story of the author's life as a child growing up in the Canal Zone. Photographs of the Canal Zone, Panama Canal, and Panama.

Tailor of Panama by John le Carré, Ballantine Books,

1996. Thriller set in Panama, revolving around a plot to annul the Panama Canal treaties.

AUDIO/VIDEO

Tailor of Panama by John le Carré, audio cassette, Random House, 1996.

Panama Canal, Modern Marvels, VHS tape, A&E Home Video, 1995. Documentary detailing the drama of the construction of the Panama Canal, 50 minutes.

WEB SITES

The best site on the Panama Canal:

The Panama Canal Commission

http://www.pananet.com/pancanal/pcc.htm

Other web sites on Panama and the canal:

1997 CIA World Factbook—Panama

http://www.odci.gov/cia/publications/factbook/pm.html

U.S. Library of Congress

http://lcweb2.loc.gov/frd/cs/patoc.html

U.S. State Department

http://www.state.gov/www/background_notes/panama_0398_bgn.html

LatinWorld (links to Latin American topics)

http://www.latinworld.com/countries/panama In Spanish and English.

Smithsonian Tropical Research Institute—Panama

http://www.si.edu/organiza/centers/stri/stri.htm In English and Spanish.

INDEX

italics indicates illustration

Alfaro, Ricardo, 55
Allen, James B., 89
Alliance for Progress, 62–63
American Conservative Union, 87
American Institute of Merchant
    Shippers, 87
Ancon, 47
Ancon Hill, 9–10, 31, 111
Ancon Hospital, 42
Arias, Arnulfo, 71
Arias, Pancho, 56, 60
Arias, Ricardo, 60

Baker, Howard, 84, 88, 91, 95
Baker, D. Newton, 52
Balboa High School, 63–64, 98
Balboa, Vasco, 25
Balladares, Ernesto Pérez, 18,19,
    107, 108, 109–110
Battle of the Levels, 42–43
Battle of the Routes, 34–36
Bennet, Douglas, 86
Bethancourt, Rómulo Escobar, 84
Bridge of the Americas, 59, *59*
Brown v. *Board of Education,* 60
Brown, Harold, 87
Bunau-Varilla, Philippe, 35, 36,
    38, 39–40
Bunker, Ellsworth, 73–77, 79, 86
Bush, George, 101, 102, 103, 105
Byrd, Robert, 88, 91, 92, 93, 95

Calderón, Ricardo Arias, 102
Canal Zone, 20, 21, *53,* 68–69, 72
    disease control in, 41–42
    flag riots in, 61–67, *65*
    life in, 48–52, *51*
    operation of, 49–55

schooling in, 51, 59–60
transfer to Panama, 9–11, 16,
    96–98, *97*
treaty terms relating to,
    74–77, 80–83
working conditions in, 52–54,
    56–59, 69
Cartagena, 38
Carter, Jimmy, 71, 79–82, 83, 85,
    88–89, 91–95, *94,* 103
Chagres River, 24, 29, 43
Chiari, Roberto, 66–67
Church, Frank, 90, 92
Citizens for the Republic, 87
Colombia, 16, 18, 26, *27,* 28,
    32–33, 36–39, 41, 99
Colón, *7,* 14, 15, 29, 38–39, 40,
    41, 51, 55, 66, *108*
Committee for the Survival of a
    Free Congress, 87
Committee of Americans for the
    Canal Treaties, 86
Congress of Industrial
    Organizations, 58
Conservative Caucus, 87
Costa Rica, *27,* 54
Council for National Defense, 87
Council of the Americas, 87
Cranston, Alan, 90
Culebra Cut, 29, *30,* 43, 44, *see
    also* Gaillard Cut
Curtis, Carl, 90

Davis, George W., 41
de la Guardia, Ricardo Adolfo, 56
de Lesseps, Ferdinand, 23, 28,
    29, 30, 31, 35
DeConcini, Dennis, 91–92

dynamite, 31, 41, 44, 45

Eisenhower, Dwight, 62, 63
Endara, Guillermo, 100, 101, 102, 106, 107

flag riots, 61–67, 65, 69, 77, 98
Florez, Florencio, *97*
Ford, Gerald, 77, 78, 79, 81, 86
Ford, Guillermo, 102

Gaillard Cut, 46, *see also* Culebra Cut
Gaillard, David, 46
Garrison, Lindley, 48
Gatun Dam, 24, 44, 46
Gatun Lake, *7*, 24
Gatun Locks, *7*, *79*
Goethals, George W., 44, 47
gold workers, 50, 51
Good Neighbor Policy, 55
Gorgas, William Crawford, 41–42
Graham, Daniel O., 88
Grant, Ulysses S., 33
Great Depression, 56
Griffin, Robert, 93

Hanna, Marcus, 35
Harding, Chester, 53
Hay, John, 37, 39–40
Herrán, Dr. Tomás, 37
Hubbard, John, 38

Interoceanic Regional Authority, 111
Isthmian Canal Commission, 33–35

Johnson, Lyndon, 64, 66–68, *68*, 70, 74, 81

Kennedy, John F., 62–63
Kissinger, Henry, 73, 75, 81, 86

Lakas, Demetrios, 72
Latin America, 21, 39, 54–55, 57, 62, 73, 80, 87, 88, 90, 95, 98, 103, 108
Laxalt, Paul, 91
Leadership Amendments, 91, 92
Linowitz, Sol M., 79, 86
local rate, 58, 63

Maine, 33
malaria, 20, 26, 30, 31, 41, 42, 48
Martyrs' Day, 98
McCain, John S. Jr., 88
McKinley, William, 32
Melville, Barbara, 72, 109, 110, *110*
Melville, Robert, 20, 72, 107, 110
Millet, Richard, 18
Miraflores Locks, *7*, 46, 85, *85*, 89, *89*
Mondale, Walter, 96–97, *97*
Monroe Doctrine, 27
Moore, Frank B., 86
Moorer, Thomas H., 88
Moreno, Miguel Jr., 61
Morgan, Henry, 25
Morison, George, 34, 35
mosquitoes, 20, 30, 41–42
Moynihan, Daniel, 90

Nashville, 38–39
Nasser, 15
National Chamber of Commerce, 87
National Public Radio, 90, 91
New Directions, 86
Nicaragua, 26–27, *27*, 33–37, *34*, 55, 99
Nixon, Richard, 72, 73, 77, 81
Noriega, Manuel, 18, 19, 72, 96, 99–103, *100*, 107, 108
Nunn, Sam, 91–92

Nutting, Wallace, 10, 20, *21*, 22, 96, *97*, 98, 99, 111

Operation Just Cause, 96, 105, *see also* Panama, invasion of
Oregon, 33
Organization of American States, 61, 66, 80, 104–105

Panama Canal, 7, *7*, *8*, 9, 12, *15*, 17, 19, 22, *24*, 32, 35–36, 38, 39, 57, 58, 61, 67, 68–70, 71, 73, 74, *75*, 76, 77, 78, *79*, 81, 82, 83–85, *85*, 88, *89*, 90, 91, 95, 97, 101, 102, 106, 109, 111
  building of by U.S., 23–25, 41, 43–46, *45*
  cost of, 31, 40, 41, 46
  defense of, 12, 16–17, 48, 50, 56, 76–80, 82, 84–85, 92, 103
  French efforts to build, 28–31
  lock vs. sea-level canal, 29, 42–43
  opening of, 47–48
  revenue from, 12–13, *13*, *15*, 82
  role of disease, 30–31, 41–42
  transfer to Panama, 11–22, 109–111
Panama Canal Authority, 16, 18–19
Panama Canal Commission, 7, 12, 13, 16, 19, 68, 69, 81
Panama Canal Company (French), 28, 30, 31, 35–36, 41
Panama Canal Company (U.S.), 16, 17, 50, 56
Panama Canal Truth Squad, 87–88
Panama Canal West Indian Employees Association, 58

Panama City, *7*, *8*, 9, 15, 25, 29, 38, 40–42, 51, 54, 55, 64, 65, 66, 72, 94, 95, 101–102, *102*, 104–108, *104*
Panama Railroad, 26, 30, 35
Panama, Republic of, *8*, 9–10, 39–41, 42–43, 52, 58, 59, 71–72, 96–97, *97*, *104*, 109–111
  and 1977 treaties, 74–77, 78, 80, 82, 84–86, 89–90, 92–95
  canal construction in, 23–25, 28–31, *30*, 43–46, *45*
  difficulties facing, 15–20, 108–109
  economy, 14, 15–16, 22, *22*, 56, 98–99, 106–107, 108–109
  invasion of by U.S., 14, 96, 101–107, *104*
  preparations for canal transfer, 11–22, 111
  relations with U.S., 39–41, 49, 54– 60, 61–70, 72–73, 98, 100–101
  revolution of, 37–39
  selection of canal route in, 25–28, *27*, 33–36
Panamanian Legislative Assembly, 19
Panamanian National Assembly, 57, 99, 101, *see also* Panamanian Legislative Assembly
Panamanian National Guard, 54, 66, 71, 72, 97, 99
Posey, Carl, 20, 47, 52
Powell, Jody, 86

Reagan, Ronald, 78, 83, 87, 93, 95
Reeder, Joe, 16
Remón, José, 58, 60
Revolutionary Democratic party (PRD), 19, 99, 108

Ritter, Jorge, 19
Robles, Marcos, 67
Rogers, William, 81
Roosevelt, Franklin D., 55
Roosevelt, Theodore, 32, 35, 36, 37, 39, 40, 43, 44, *45*, 46, 89
Royo, Arístedes, 97, *97*, 99

Schecter, Gerald, 86
Shaler, James, 38
silver workers, 50–52, *53*, 57, 121
Snyder, Marion Gene, 77
Solis, Galileo, 63
Spanish American War, 32, 33
Spooner Act, 35–36
Spooner, John C., 35
Statement of Understanding, 85, 88, 91, *see also* Leadership Amendments
Stennis, John, 91
Stevens, John, 42, 43, 44
Suez Canal, 14, 24, 28

Tack, Juan Antonio, 73, 75–76
Tack-Kissinger Statement of Principles, 75–76
Thurmond, Strom, 77
Torrijos, Omar, 71–73, 78, 80, 82, 85, 88, 92–95, *94*, 99, 103
Trans-Isthmus railroad, 20
treaties
    Clayton-Bulwer Treaty, 27, 33–34
    Hay-Bunau-VarillaTreaty, 39–40, 49, 54, 55, 61, 63, 66–67, 75, 81
    Hay-Herrán Treaty, 37
    Hay-Pauncefort Treaty, 34
    Hull-Alfaro treaty, 55
    negotiation of 1977 treaties, 72–80
    Neutrality Treaty, 12, 16–17, 82, 84, 88–92, 94, 97, 103–104
    Panama Canal Treaty of 1955, 58–59
    Panama Canal Treaty of 1977, 9, 12, 16–17, 80–93, 94, 95, 97, 98, 110–111

United Nations, 63, 73, 104
U.S. Defense Department, 74, 77–78, 87
U.S. House, 36, 43, 77, 84, 87
U.S. rate, 58, 63
U.S. Senate, 9, 35–37, 43, 55, 77, 83–87
    and ratification of Hay-Bunau-Varilla Treaty, 40
    and ratification of Panama Canal treaties of 1977, 88–93
U.S. Southern Command, 9, 20, 21, 50, 96
U.S. State Department, 74, 77, 86

Vance, Cyrus, 81, 86
volcanoes, 36

Wallace, John, 41–43
West Indian workers, 29, 41, 49, 50–51, 52–54, *53*, 56
West Indies, 24, 29, 36, 43
World War I, 48, 79
World War II, 16, 56–57, 60, 79
Wyse, Lucien Napoleon-Bonaparte, 28

yellow fever, 20, 26, 30–31, 41–42, 48
Young Republicans, 87

Zubieta, Alberto Aleman, 16